Trojan Horses

Trojan Horses

SAVING THE CLASSICS FROM CONSERVATIVES

Page duBois

NEW YORK UNIVERSITY PRESS

New York and London

NEW YORK UNIVERSITY PRESS
New York and London

© 2001 by New York University
All rights reserved

Library of Congress Cataloging-in-Publication Data
duBois, Page.
Trojan horses : saving the classics from conservatives /
Page duBois.
p.   cm.
Includes bibliographical references and index.
ISBN 0-8147-1946-5 (acid-free paper)
1. Classical philology—Study and teaching—United States.
2. Civilization, Classical—Study and teaching—United States.
3. Classical literature—History and criticism—Thoery, etc.
4. Education—Political aspects—United States. 5. Education,
Humanistic—United States. 6. Conservatism—United States.
I. Title.
PA78.U6 D83 2001
880.9'001—dc21   00-012244

10 9 8 7 6 5 4 3 2 1

for John Daley

Contents

Trojan Horses

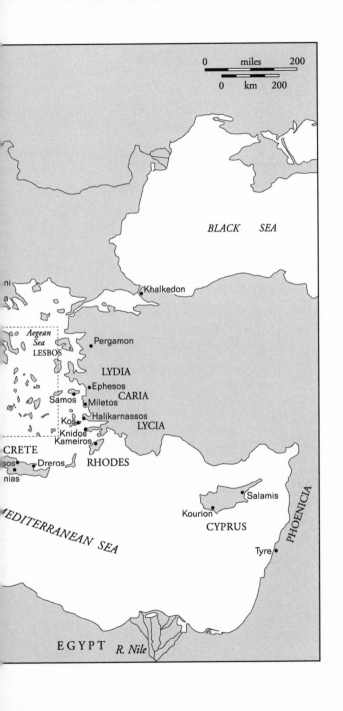

1

Whose Greeks?

> What can't be exhausted is the always-new adjustment every age makes to the classical world, measuring itself against it. If we set the classicist the task of understanding *his own* age better by means of antiquity, then his task has no end.
> —Nietzsche, "We Classicists"

I believe that reading ancient Greek art and culture can illuminate and enrich our present circumstances, but also that the Greeks were far stranger, more complicated, and more ambiguous than they might appear in much that circulates about them in the current climate. There is more to know, and much more to say about our relationship to the past of classical antiquity. The interpretation of the Greek and Roman classics, rather than dead, as some alarmists claim, remains as always a contested field, one in which conflicting interpretations clash, one about which I want to have my say here.

Americans are witnessing a resurgence of interest in the classics. Garry Wills discussed this phenomenon in an article in the *New York Times Magazine* (February 16, 1997), calling attention to a rising tide of books, films, and television programs devoted to the ancient Greeks and Romans. We have seen the success of a television series on the deeds of the mythological Greek hero Hercules, and a miniseries version of Homer's *Odyssey*. The television program "Xena, Warrior Princess," features a heroine modeled on the ancient myth of the Amazons, like Wonder Woman before her. Disney has released an animated feature film on Hercules, and followed it with stage shows and spectacles at various Disneylands and -worlds. Best-sellers recount the myths and legends of classical antiquity. Self-help books point to the ancient gods and goddesses as timeless paradigms of human character. At the beginning of the twenty-first century, people continue to be fascinated by the remnants of the cultures of ancient Greece and Rome, two millenia distant in time.

Enrolled in my course in classical mythology are students of literature and the classics, but also students majoring in political science, animal physiology, cellular biology, art history, general biology, structural engineering, physics, economics, human development, history, ecology, media, and anthropology. These students come from many cultural and ethnic backgrounds. They don't have to take this course; it doesn't fulfill requirements for their majors. But they are nonetheless curious about the stories of ancient Greek heroes and gods, of Helen, of the wooden horse that smuggled the Greek heroes into the city of Troy, of Herakles—as the Greeks called

Hercules—and of Persephone, the daughter of Demeter seized by the god of the dead, who ate a pomegranate seed in the underworld and was required forever to spend a third of the year with her husband in the world of the dead, while her mother mourned above and brought winter to the earth.

I want to share with contemporary readers, many of whom read the myths of the ancient Greeks in school long or not so long ago, the variety within ancient Greek culture, its fascinating practices in the domains of politics, sexuality, and religion. There is much new scholarship in these fields, some of which is listed at the end of this book, and I would like more people to know another version of the Greeks from that often promoted in the popular press. Among other things, some of these Greeks thought women had dangerously powerful sexual drives, that the public allusion to sexual positions was comic, and that homoeroticism was one of the gifts of Aphrodite. These Greeks participated in a radical democracy, one in which each citizen had a right to speak and vote without being represented by an elder or a better, and in which the citizens themselves made all political decisions. These Greeks inhabited a world full of gods, where Hermes protected the boundaries of their property and their states, and guided them into the underworld when they died, where the god Dionysos was in the wine they drank, where drinking wine,

Dionysos's gift to human beings, was an act of worship, and where the actors in the dionysiac theater were possessed by the god.

I'm alarmed because I see in the popular press these same Greeks and their stories travestied by those who want to justify their political platform for America by means of a slanted, polemical appeal to the Western past, by a reductive, one-dimensional, shallow interpretation of Greek and Roman civilization. I think of William Bennett's *Book of Virtues* and Allan Bloom's *The Closing of the American Mind,* among others. These contemporary writers use the Greeks to argue for their views. Their positions lend implicit support to politicians and religious leaders who advocate so-called family values, restriction of women to their homes and the requirement of obedience to their husbands, and the dissolution of separation between Christianity and the state, while arguing for homophobia, militarism, xenophobia, and the restriction of immigration. Still other scholars sound the death knell of the study of antiquity, blaming those they call "multiculturalists," that is, all those who disagree with them about politics in the present. I fear not only that such arguments will succeed in communicating their monolithic and polemically reductive ideas of the ancient world to readers, but also that classics as a field will wither like Egyptology because of its association with such reactionary ideas. As a friend of mine said, "They're right that we should read the Greeks, but for all the wrong reasons."

Let me begin with the story of Daedalus, the first human being to fly, whose story is, like so many Greek myths, full of violence, bestiality, and strangeness:

The mythical Daedalus descended from Hephaistos, god of smiths. Once upon a time Hephaistos conceived desire for the virgin goddess of Athens, Athena, and tried to rape her. She fought him off, and in the process he ejaculated on her cloak. Athena brushed off her garment with a bit of wool, let it fall to the ground, and thus fertilized the earth, the goddess Gaia, with the smith god's seed. From this union were born the Athenian people. The storytellers trace the lineage of Daedalus back to this scene; the Athenians come from this moment of violence, and belong to their own land in a way like no other people. They called themselves "autochthonous," born from the earth itself. The Greeks named Daedalus's own father both "Eupalamus," "Skilled of hand," and Metion, "Man of cunning intelligence," to mark Daedalus's ingenuity and dexterity. The Athenian Socrates, teacher of Plato at the very beginnings of philosophy, himself the son of a stonemason, traced his family line back to Daedalus.

According to legend, Daedalus killed his nephew, perhaps jealous because the nephew, who invented the saw, was even more skillful than he. After that, Daedalus fled Athens and moved to the island of Crete, situated in the middle of the Aegean Sea between mainland Greece and Africa, to serve its king. Daedalus had already become *the* maker, the first human being to invent and fashion many beautiful and useful things that enable and adorn civilization—elaborate jewelry, statues, weapons, and armor. He created marvels on Crete. His name first appears in Homer's *Iliad* as the maker of a dancing floor for Ariadne, daughter of King Minos of Crete. His story here gets tangled up in the plentiful store of legends concerning this Mediterranean island, a center of civilization long before the Greeks became powerful, an island marked by its ancient connections with Asia and Africa.

King Minos of Crete was a descendant of Zeus, greatest of the Olympian gods. Zeus, in one of his many unions with mortals of both sexes, seduced Europa, daughter of the king of Tyre, in Asia Minor, appearing before her on the beach in the form of a charming little white bull. Europa was so enchanted by the beauty of this bull that she mounted on his back, "his softness fooling her," as the poet Charles Olson says. Zeus carried her off to Crete, where she gave her name to the continent of Europe. There she gave birth to Minos, who in his turn married Pasiphae, daughter of the sun, and she bore him several children, among them a daughter, Ariadne. One day Minos prayed to Poseidon, god of the sea, who sent another beautiful bull from the sea, this time for sacrifice; Minos found the bull so lovely that he could not kill it, even to please the god. Poseidon, in revenge for this slight, caused Minos's wife Pasiphae to conceive lust for this bull. She appealed to Daedalus, and he constructed an elaborate disguise for her, so that the bull, believing her to be a cow, mounted the queen and had intercourse with her. Impregnated by the bull, Pasiphae gave birth to the Minotaur, a monster, half bull and half human. Horrified, the Cretans asked Daedalus to hide this hideous offspring away forever from human sight. He built a maze, the infamous labyrinth, and concealed the Minotaur at its heart.

After a time the Athenian hero Theseus arrived on Crete, one of an annual shipment of twelve Athenian youth, six boys and six girls sent as tribute to the Cretans, who planned to sacrifice them to the Minotaur. But Theseus escaped death by winning the heart of Ariadne, Minos's daughter, the girl of the Homeric dancing floor. She persuaded Daedalus to help her save Theseus from being devoured by the monster. The maker of the maze gave her a thread, which she passed on to Theseus, telling him to fasten it at the mouth of the labyrinth, and to unwind it as he moved inside. He found the Minotaur at its center, killed him, then wound the thread back to the entrance.

Daedalus, with his ingenious schemes aiding the women of Minos's house, had angered the king, who imprisoned him on the island along with his son Icarus. Unhappy in his subjection, Daedalus hatched a plan for the two of them to escape from Crete. In the Roman poet Ovid's account of his story, Daedalus says that King Minos blocked his escape on land and sea, but the sky still remained open: The king was unable to control the sky above them. In Ovid's telling, Daedalus changed the laws of nature by taking to the air. He laid out feathers, attached them in graduated sizes with thread and wax, bent and curved them so that they resembled the wings of birds. Before take-off he warned his son Icarus to fly a middle course between the sun and the water, and they rose on their brilliant wings and flew. Those below, a shepherd and a plowman, looked up in amazement at their flight. But Icarus daringly flew too close to the sun, the wax melted, his feathers failed, and he fell into the sea and drowned.

When Vergil's great hero Aeneas, survivor of the ruined city Troy and founder of Rome, arrived in Italy, he found a set of doors made by Daedalus in the land of the Cumaean Sibyl. They marked the spot where Daedalus first landed on his solo flight from Crete, having lost his son to the sea. The architect had built a great temple to Apollo there, in thanks for his own safe arrival, and left his marvelous wings as an offering to the god. He depicted his own story on the temple's doors, in a version that recalls Aeneas's own disastrous dalliance in Africa with the queen of Carthage, Dido:

> Here can be seen the loving of the savage bull and Pasiphae laid out to receive it and deceive her husband Minos. Here too is the hybrid offspring, the Minotaur, half-man and half-animal, the memorial to a perverted love, and here is its home, built with such great labor, the inextricable Labyrinth. But Daedalus takes pity on the great love of the princess Ariadne and unravels the winding paths of his own baffling maze, guiding the blind steps of Theseus with a thread.

In Vergil's account, the mourning artist Daedalus had tried to depict the fall of his son Icarus on this work of art, but his hands had fallen, helpless. Soon Aeneas himself descended into the labyrinth of the underworld, into the land of the dead, in order to encounter past and future, to visit his dead father and see Dido and his heirs still to be born. He carried a marvelous golden bough as a talisman to protect him and guarantee his safe return to the land of the living.

The legendary Daedalus was the first human artisan, carpenter, sculptor, engineer, architect, builder, pilot, and artist. The adjective associated with his name, *daidaleos,* probably the root and origin of his name, was associated from earliest times with highly worked armor, jewels, vessels, musical instruments, ships, and furniture. The Greeks and Romans admired him as the inventor of carpentry, of the axe, the auger, glue, and the masts of boats; he was said to have built many of the most ancient temples in the Greek world, and to have made wonderful wooden statues capable of opening their eyes, walking, and moving their arms. His genius made him almost divine, capable of turning inanimate wooden images into animate, mobile creatures.

Poets in antiquity retold the story of Daedalus countless times. It was passed on to our own day in the visual arts as well as in literature by, among others, the painter Brueghel, who showed the fall of Icarus in a painting's background, with a heedless plowman at the center of his canvas. This painting in turn inspired the twentieth-century poet W. H. Auden, who described that fall in his poem "Musée des Beaux Arts." Auden wrote about how the "Old Masters," painters like Brueghel, understood suffering, which "takes place/ While someone else is eating or opening a window or just walking dully along." Auden describes Brueghel's *Icarus,* how the plowman hears the splash and the cry of Icarus's fall, but how "for him it was not an important failure."

> *. . . the expensive delicate ship that must have seen*
> *Something amazing, a boy falling out of the sky,*
> *Had somewhere to get to and sailed calmly on.*

The poem uses the painting's record of Icarus's fall as an emblem for everyday life's indifference to martyrdom and suffering or the miraculous human flight, great dramas witnessed casually by human beings going about their mundane and necessary business. In the twentieth century the story of Daedalus inspired many interpretations and rewritings. The hero of James Joyce's autobiographical novel *Portrait of the Artist as a Young Man* is Stephen Daedalus. This Daedalus also moves through a single day of Dublin life in Joyce's labyrinthine masterpiece *Ulysses.*

The ancient story remains rich in significance for understanding classical civilization. It responds to questions the ancients asked themselves, the implications of which endure in Western culture. How did human beings come into existence? Are we the descendants of gods, born from the earth, autochthonous, like plants? Who invented all the techniques, the skills, and sciences that separate us from the animals? Why is it that some human beings have what seem incredible, almost inhuman talents? How is it that most of us have sex only among ourselves, and not with animals? What civilizations preceded the Greeks' and the Romans'? The story points to connections between the Greeks and Asia, the Near East of Tyre, and between the Greeks and Romans and Africa, so close to the southern coast of Crete, so crucial to Roman history. The story presents the passage of ancient Greek culture westward, from ancient Tyre, home of Minos's mother, to Crete, to Italy. It touches on the theme of the extraordinary man, the person of uncommon skill, and also on the anonymity of thousands of craftsmen, architects, and sculptors, workers whose names will forever be lost to history and for whom Daedalus stands. Daedalus's story reminds us of both the generosity and the indifference of the ancient gods. It recalls the special status of the Athenians, born from the artisan god Hephaistos and the primeval goddess Earth, and the invention of philosophy in Athens. The daring of Icarus reminds us of the classical Athenians' fears, expressed in Greek tragedy, of those who strove and achieved too much, likening themselves to gods, in danger of attracting the gods' jealous attention, and in need of control by their fellow citizens. The myth touches on the theme of paternal authority, the vexed relationship between fathers and sons echoed in other myths like that of Oedipus. The story includes murder, adultery, bestiality, the impossibility and the even more fantastic possibility of human flight, the relationship between master and servant, king and architect, the death of a son and the father's responsibility for the risks that led to this great loss, mourning and recovery from mourning. It is a celebration of human ingenuity and a meditation as well on the costs of that ingenuity.

And yet, in the best-seller *The Book of Virtues: A Treasury of Great Moral Stories,* tales for those destined to be trained in his conception of virtue, William Bennett tells a painfully narrow and reduced version of the story of Daedalus, this first artist. Most of the story is elided in Bennett's account. Bennett retells only the story of

Daedalus's and Icarus's flight, which he glosses ponderously; in his view, the point of this great and elaborate myth is that Icarus, who flew too close to the sun, was disobedient, a bad boy who deserved his unhappy fate.

After recounting the episode of the flight and fall, he concludes:

> This famous Greek myth reminds us exactly why young people have a responsibility to obey their parents—for the same good reason parents have a responsibility to guide their children: there are many things adults know that young people do not. . . . Safe childhoods and successful upbringings require a measure of obedience, as Icarus finds out the hard way.[1]

Bennett underlines his moral with this praise of obedience coupled with a threat of disaster for the disobedient. The elaborate mythical narrative, so abundant in themes of significance for understanding the Greeks and ourselves, is reduced to a moralizing parable and subordinated to Bennett's message about hierarchy and so-called family values: The son must obey the father. Bennett stresses obedience to authority in this text, yet fails to acknowledge that Daedalus in his turn exhibited disobedience as he defied the commands of his master King Minos. Even the truncated mythic episode explores the limits of authority and of paternalism. And it also celebrates the yearning for free flight even as it expresses anxiety at the prospect of flying free. In Bennett's account there is no awareness of the wealth of meanings in this reduced fragment of the myth, of the story's exploration of human beings' paradoxical needs for freedom and security, no mention of the celebration of human skill and ingenuity, questions of power, audacity, and genius, of the father's disobedience of King Minos, and of Daedalus's great loss and mourning. Even as an interpretation of this tiny morsel of the myth of Daedalus, Bennett's moral appears strikingly inadequate. In Bennett's book, full of stories mostly "drawn from the corpus of Western civilization" (15), the "great moral story" of Daedalus and Icarus appears in the section called "Responsibility," one of those traditional values that the former drug czar and Secretary of Education seeks to instill in Americans. Responsibility, resembling his other categories Work, Perseverance, and Self-Discipline, requires first and foremost obedience to one's superiors.

In a further development of his pedagogical mission, Bennett's stories, reissued in a special edition for children, have been shown in animated form on television. And on PBS, often the target of Bennett's vigorous fulminations against its public funding: "When I learned about [the PBS involvement], I chuckled, because people know that I'm a critic of public funding of television."[2] The television program is preceded by an announcement that Cigna, the Arthur Vining Davis Foundation, and the Olin Foundation contributed funding. The televised tales of virtue, animated not in

Bennett's West, but in Korea, are framed by the continuing story of two children, Zack and Annie, who confront problems of virtue in everyday life. They are guided, incongruously, by a buffalo with a deep voice called "Plato," a figure for Bennett himself. His companions are a bobcat, "Soc," for Socrates, resembling Sylvester ("I t'ot I taw a puddytat") the Cat, and a prairie dog named "Ari," for Aristotle—thus have the mighty of Western philosophy fallen. These male personages are joined by a female red-tailed hawk, for no apparent reason but gender diversity, named "Aurora," or dawn. The feminine principle guides us ever upward. The buffalo is clearly in charge. He is huge and manly, boasting horns and thick black eyebrows.

In the program on Responsibility, the girl Annie encounters a problem about some cakes baked by her mother, cakes she had promised to deliver but dropped because she was led astray by a friend on a bicycle. The buffalo counsels her in his deep voice, and reads to her from his book the exemplary stories of England's King Alfred, who failed to watch a peasant woman's cakes and let them burn ("leadership and responsibility go hand in hand," says the buffalo), and of an old woman (English, again) who must lure her greedy children into caring for her by deceiving them with a locked treasure chest that they discover, after her death, contains nothing but broken glass. The buffalo also solemnly reads the tale of Icarus and his father Daedalus. In the animated version of the Icarus story, the father's voice is that of John Forsythe, familiar to American audiences as Blake Carrington of television's long-running prime-time soap opera, *Dynasty,* that exuberant ode to wealth and Reagan-Bush America. Here again, of course, there is no mention of the union between Pasiphae and the bull, nor of the mysteries of Minotaur and sacrifice and labyrinth, nor of Daedalus's failure to obey the authoritative commands of King Minos. The animated Daedalus is impatient and instructs his son: "You must watch and learn, listen and obey." After the boy plummets vividly into the sea, drowns, and is buried, "Plato" the buffalo moralizes portentously about the irresponsibility of the child Icarus. The son knew the danger, but chose to ignore his father's advice and paid a terrible price.

After another episode about Compassion, including the Roman story of Androcles and the lion, the evening concludes with an advertisement for Bennett's *Children's Book of Virtues,* and footage of actual, unanimated children, of various colors, saying virtuous things. The last word is spoken by a beautiful little blonde girl, who says, "without virtue, the world would be kind of like a grumpy old place without any happy people."

In *The Moral Compass,* sequel and companion to *The Book of Virtues,* Bennett again mines classical antiquity for inspiring stories, citing Hercules and Perseus, Alexander the Great and Ulysses. The section called "Standing Fast" curiously offers up the example of

Oedipus the king of Thebes—who killed his father, married his mother, and fathered children with her—who is Freud's paradigm for what he believes to be a universal desire on the male child's part to kill his father and sleep with his mother. Bennett's version cozily omits such horrors, central to the sexual history of the West in the twentieth century, and concludes that Oedipus, after having morally "stood fast" against the Sphinx, "became king of Thebes, and wisely and well did he rule, and for many a long year the land prospered."[3]

In such settings, the culture of ancient Greece is once again, as before in American culture, reduced and manipulated to persuade readers and viewers of the immemorial truth of the most illiberal of political opinions. Bennett's collections of uplifting anecdotes are an affirmation of eternal human nature and the rightness of the things already and always known to be so. "Children—and everyone else—should stand fast, and should always obey elders and betters."

The author of these widely-read anthologies is a conservative activist. William Bennett is a codirector of Empower America and the John M. Olin Distinguished Fellow in Cultural Policy Studies at the Heritage Foundation. He was a founder of the neoconservative Madison Center for Educational Affairs, once head of the National Endowment for the Humanities, fellow of the Hudson Institute, chairman of National Empowerment

Television (a project of the Free Congress Foundation), also drug czar, and Secretary of Education under conservative Republican presidents.

In this book, I want to point to some things left out of William Bennett's view of the ancient Greeks, parts of the story that are forgotten or suppressed or sanitized in order to present an ancient world that shores up and validates his political opinions of today. As we know from work on fairy tales, even children can absorb, think, and fantasize about complexities reflected in stories inherited from the past, stories that register the range of human experience and are not bowdlerized and rendered politically correct for their consumption. My presentation of the ancient Greeks seeks to restore a more complicated culture, one that is different from our own but which has human possibilities we might well remember now, that render unfamiliar some of the domestic, sexual, political, and religious arrangements we take for granted, that we sometimes believe to be grounded in eternal "human nature." I would like to bring to light some aspects of antiquity discussed in valuable recent scholarship which polemicists such as Bennett suppress in their selective appropriation of the past, in interpretations they present as timeless truth justifying a particular view of human nature and authorizing their ideas. They give us not the full range of ancient culture, its contradictions, heterogeneities, differences from, and similarities to our own, but idols

erected by themselves as victors over the rich and complicated history of ancient Greece. Theirs is a selective
and impoverished version of ancient culture, one that
for the most part erases historical difference and, looking through the window of history, finds the Greeks
motionless as in a diorama, caught in a tableau vivant
exemplifying the moral virtues of conservative twenty-
first-century America. Conservatives fetishize a particular stereotype of the Greeks by fixing and repeating it,
and they distort history for their political purposes.

We need a picture of the Greeks that is more accurate, multifaceted, and variegated than theirs. The
Greeks cannot all be lumped into a set of anecdotes
demonstrating contemporary virtues; they differed radically from one another, and were in fact notoriously
contentious. They had subtle and complicated interpretations of their own inherited myths and stories. Their
culture changed dramatically, even over the three centuries of the classical period. My survey here seeks neither to idealize nor to denigrate ancient Athens and the
ancient Greeks. The classical Athenian male citizen kept
slaves, subjected women, hated and frequently brutal-
ized his enemies, and forced slaves to work and die in
the city's mines. Ancient democracy was based on exclusion and frequently on imperial expansion, on the
Athenian state's ambitions throughout the Mediterranean world. If I stress here particular elements of
ancient Greek culture, my reading is generated as a

response to the popular press, to a version of antiquity I find unrecognizable. Ancient Greece was not a utopia, cannot be reconfigured retrospectively as an Eden for left or right. But little about the various, contradictory, heterogeneous, and polymorphic culture of the Athenians has in recent years been registered in the mass media and the popular press, and I see mine as a compensatory reading. Except for the work of Michel Foucault, David Halperin, and Jack Winkler on ancient sexuality, the important recent scholarship that has transformed many scholars' view of ancient Greek society has had little impact on most people's idea of antiquity.

It is of course impossible fully to recover ancient civilization. But we can acknowledge the interests scholars bring to their work, the ways in which their location in the present affects what they see when they look at the past. I see not sameness in antiquity, but difference and complexity, an unfamiliar world which can offer not a mirror image of ourselves, but rather a contradictory, complicated set of beginnings for Western culture. Like Bennett, I think we should study the past, but not to find nuggets of eternal wisdom. Rather we can comprehend in our history a fuller range of human possibilities, of beginnings, of error, and of difference. I believe my presentation of ancient Greek culture, though brief, is more accurate, more multifaceted, and more intricate than theirs.

I will focus on three different aspects of this culture

that recent classical scholarship has made more visible: the sexual practices of the classical period in Athens, the radical democracy of ancient Athens, and the polytheism of the ancient Greeks. In all three of these cases, the Greeks were anomalous, often strange, and different from us, not just storytellers of fables about obedience to the father.

We inhabit the present, accept it as reality, and think (except perhaps for those who read a great deal of science fiction) that this is the way things have always been, will be, and ought to be. We live in a world in which contemporary culture preoccupies many people, where any reading of ancient history may seem irrelevant. Even some academics seem to be giving up on history entirely, turning toward popular culture, with its aleatory, seemingly anarchist array of representations. Some regard American popular culture with fascinated passivity, perhaps yearning for its randomness to yield up something new. Critics invest in an expectant survey of music, television, and comic books, some with the hope that everyday life, in its rush, will produce something unexpected, some novelty, that the utopian might emerge in some incalculable way, or that some unforeseen mutation will point the way to the future, even a future of resistances that might transform experience. Hope, pleasure, or dread keep many of us transfixed in a gaze at the very near future, as if paralyzed by the machine of the world, as if it will give us something we want, something hitherto unseen.

I don't want to ally myself with those who oppose the teaching of popular culture and cultural studies. We need to know how to produce critiques of the world we live in, to analyze our own culture. Nor would I advocate a position of elitist pessimism, mourning the loss of European high culture. I believe there are resistance, pleasure, compelling interest, even utopian elements in the culture of the present. But in this present, we also need some critical relationship to other times and other places. I think we should still read the dead, among them those Greeks who not only invented philosophy and democracy and the jury system, but also kept slaves and excluded their women from political life. Their culture was diverse and heterogeneous, and we need a fuller sense of all that it offers to contemporary readers. For example, our reading of a poet like Sappho (whom I'll discuss later), a female poet at the threshold of the creation of the very idea of the writer, might allow us to see the diverse, vivid, complicated, and contradictory beginnings of Western civilizations.

One of the great rewards of reading history is the realization that things have not in fact always been the way they are now, that people in other times and places have organized human societies, of whatever size, differently. If we allow ourselves to be open to the myriad lost possibilities of historical human cultures, we amplify our present often limited sense of human potential. We can throw open the narrow window through which many people now see the ancient world, and look at much more that is recognizable in our repertory of human possibility and in our inheritance from the ancient dead.

2

Their Greeks

In this chapter, I offer some case studies of writers whose works rely on what I will argue is a narrow, reductive view of ancient Greek culture. Some of these authors, like William Bennett, rely on a cartoon version of ancient Greece to authorize their platform for contemporary America. They present a simplistic, ahistorical view of human nature, and find it everywhere. In their diorama labeled ancient history sit the Greeks, stuffed, looking just like us. Such thinking distorts, freezes, and idolizes ancient culture, representing our own time as simple repetition of a past these contemporary writers invent, often ignoring the inevitable differences produced in more than twenty-five hundred years of historical change. Their ancient Greeks serve as a fixed, immutable point of beginning, a single origin for a monolithic Western civilization now besieged by a new set of barbarians, immigrants from new continents, with other histories, seeking to displace the Greeks from their imaginary seat at the beginning, a seat sometimes but not always shared with ancient Israel.

Of course there are differences among the thinkers I will discuss in what follows. Some are professional classicists, philosophers, and historians, while others are more popular writers with an interest in classical civilization. The work of Allan Bloom, for example, consists not only of his best-selling *The Closing of the American Mind,* but also includes serious, careful work on the Platonic corpus, influenced by Leo Strauss, whose work on Plato has had important consequences for some scholars working on ancient philosophy in the United States. If the scholarly work of the writers I cite is frequently rigorous, careful, and scrupulous, they nonetheless seem to concur on the reductive portrait of the ancient Greeks they polemically offer to a popular audience.

Several of the authors I will discuss received support from the conservative John M. Olin Foundation for the writing and publication of their work. As Jon Wiener points out:

> Olin and several smaller foundations provide a vital link between universities and the political world of Republicans in government, right-wing think tanks and conservative publications. . . . They buy time off from teaching for conservative scholars to develop arguments justifying right-wing policies, and then help put those ideas into the public discourse, where they can do conservatives some good.[4]

Eric Alterman, in "The Troves of Academe," also published in *The Nation,* reports: "The usual Olin method
is to pick a particularly distinguished right-wing member of a given humanities or social sciences faculty and
shower him with millions in salary, research moneys and
student fellowships. . . . The late Allan Bloom received
more than $3.5 million at the University of Chicago."
Ellen Messer-Davidow has written on the massive conservative apparatus of think tanks, training programs,
foundations, and other institutions. She describes the
move toward *cultural* conservatism after the election of
Ronald Reagan in 1980: "cultural conservatives, according to William Lind, 'seek to conserve traditional Western culture' because it 'is functionally true,' that is, 'it is
necessary if our society is to be successful.'" There is "a
necessary, unbreakable and causal relationship between
traditional Western, Judeo-Christian values, definitions
of right and wrong, ways of thinking and ways of living
. . . and the secular success of Western societies" (46).
Cultural conservatives have sought to make their presence felt in conservative think tanks and academic institutions, to make higher education a "free-market econ-
omy." Neoconservative groups like the Olin Foundation
support journals like the *American Spectator* and the
National Review, the Madison Center, the National Association of Scholars, and the Heritage Foundation,
which in 1991 had a budget of $19.3 million.

◆

In 1987 Allan Bloom published the best-selling *The Closing of the American Mind: How Higher Education Has Failed Democracy and Impoverished the Souls of Today's Students,* an extended complaint about the state of American education and society, and began a wave of polemical conservative commentary on the university, the curriculum, and the lessons to be learned from the Greeks. He detected similarities between today's youth and the ancient Athenian democratic young found wanting by his favored ancient Greek philosopher, Plato. Faced with our young, Bloom lamented:

> Not only are they free to decide their place, but they are also free to decide whether they will believe in God or be atheists, or leave their options open by being agnostic; whether they will be straight or gay, or, again, keep their options open; whether they will marry and whether they will stay married; whether they will have children—and so on endlessly. There is no necessity, no morality, no social pressure, no sacrifice to be made that militates going in or turning away from any of these directions.[5]

Bloom was distressed by the unfortunate multiplicity of choices open to his students. In contrast to the vacillating weakness of contemporary university students, the disciples of Plato, according to Bloom, had a passion for "political glory" (329). After describing in detail the contrast, which reflected badly on the twentieth century, he concluded: "The aspiration to be number one and gain great fame is both natural in man and, properly trained, one of the soul's great strengths. Democracy in itself is hostile to such spiritedness and prevents its fulfillment" (329). Bloom shared the ancient philosopher Plato's disdain for democratic governance and its effects on citizens, and seemed to believe that democracy itself goes against human nature.

Bloom also disapproved of the gender arrangements of the present, making a plea for old-fashioned "female modesty":

> Modesty in the old dispensation was *the* female virtue, because it governed the powerful desire that related men to women, providing a gratification in harmony with the procreation and rearing of children, the risk and responsibility of which fell naturally—that is, biologically—on women. Although modesty impeded sexual intercourse, its result was to make such gratification central to a serious life and to enhance the delicate interplay between the sexes, which makes acquiescence of the will as important as possession of the body. (101–2)

Bloom found fault with youth, with education, with gender arrangements, with politics in the present, and discovered a lost golden age in the Academy of the philosopher Plato. He recalled much to praise in a past distinguished by female modesty, and neglected entirely to mention that Plato lived in a world of male lovers. In a cryptic allusion to ancient pederasty, Bloom isolated Plato from his culture and recalled the *Phaedrus* when discussing Thomas Mann's *Death in Venice,* only to sanitize the practices of homoeroticism in the ancient city: "Plato found a way of expressing and beautifying, of sublimating, perverse sexuality" (237). In our culture, in contrast, eros is "meaningless and low" (237).

Bloom's best-selling book began a trend in critiques of the university and its role in modern society. Conservative writers joined him in lamenting the state of education and other domains of modern life. One of these conservative thinkers is Donald Kagan, author of *ON THE ORIGINS OF WAR and the Preservation of Peace,* which intervenes in debates about the history of war and the place of the military in contemporary societies.[6] The cover of the paperback edition of this book presents an interesting aspect, since the question of the origins of war is prominently displayed, and the preservation of peace is typographically subordinated to one sixth the size of the former. The blurbs on the back offer praise from *The New Criterion* and from George P. Shultz, former U.S. Secretary of State, who remarks that "[R]ecent events regrettably confirm that warfare is inherent to any system of world affairs yet imagined, so we had better do all we can to prevent it." The ostensible purpose of this volume is to prevent war, yet it betrays a belief in the unchanging nature of human society, its essential propensity to violence and war, and presents, based on a historical survey, the argument that the only way to preserve the peace is to prepare for war. From this point of view, we need militarism and strong leaders capable of implementing it.

Kagan proceeds through several disparate narratives of events leading up to wars, in an idiosyncratic order: first the Peloponnesian (431–404 B.C.E.), then the First World War (1914–1918), followed by the Second Punic (218–201 B.C.E.) and the Second World War (1939–1945). Finally he provides a narrative describing the narrow averting of war during the Cuban missile crisis (1962). His account has many remarkable features. First of all, to present these narratives in the order in which he does skews their chronology dramatically. He gives a profoundly partisan view of history as undifferentiated, as centuries of repetition. The ancient histories are interspersed between the modern ones, giving the impression that we are dealing here with human universals. The ancient world is identical to the modern, even interchangeable with it, in the ways that count. His analysis and interpretations of the causes and conduct of the ancient wars, the Peloponnesian War between the Athenians and the Spartans, and the Punic War, between the Carthaginians and the Romans, provide the founding categories for his understanding of all history then and since.

Kagan is really a war buff, not a peacemonger. He is fascinated by war, observing with a certain contentment that the world has been at war for a greater proportion of history than it has been at peace. His protestations that the avoidance of war is possible and necessary, and that this is the aim of his text, are unconvincing. "War" is made an absolute category; all its occurrences are homogenized, with little recognition of differences over the huge period of history from 431 B.C.E. to 1962 C.E., a span of almost twenty-four hundred years, in which we might imagine that much had changed, including the very idea of war itself. In this view, the human condition, like war, is nearly immutable: "war is probably part of the human condition and likely to be with us for some time yet" (569). Because of this, we need strong states and strong leaders committed to "peacekeeping," that is, militarism and domination by those strong states led by strong leaders. He focuses on powerful men in his narratives of historical events, and he personifies the states they led, attributing to them universal, eternal human attributes: the Roman Republic, for example, is called "arrogant and careless" (570). He expresses, seemingly with regret, concern about that unfortunate incident recorded in the New Testament, the Sermon on the Mount, in which Jesus urged on his followers love over retribution, an episode which has led to a lot of what Kagan intimates is unrelieved cowardice.

> The martial values and the respect for power have not entirely disappeared, but they have been overlayed [sic] by other ideas and values, some of them unknown to the classical republics. The most important of these is

the Judeo-Christian tradition, and especially the paci-
fist strain of Christianity that emphasizes the Sermon
on the Mount rather than the more militant strain that
played so large a role over the centuries. (571)

The careless lumping together of the Judaic and the
Christian traditions aside, in a phrase which elides the
militancy and violence to which Christians indeed subjected Jews for centuries, regret and nostalgia here are
unmistakable. Kagan concludes that peace will only be
preserved "by maintaining a strong military power and
the willingness to use it when necessary" (573). His is the
doctrine of "peace through strength" (414).

Pacific or isolationist states are represented as weak,
implicitly cowardly, and unmanly. Kagan cites with approval Correlli Barnett's characterization of British military leaders of the nineteen thirties as "Cassandras in
gold braid" (417). They were fearful of war, therefore ef-
feminate, and feminized. Kagan seems to forget that the
Cassandra of ancient Greek myth always prophesied the
truth. In his view, real men, real leaders, and powerful
states have an obligation to keep the peace, and are mo-
tivated not by economic motives, as Marxists suggest,
but by the cause of "honor." Kennedy caused the Cuban
missile crisis by his unseemly vacillations; disaster was
averted only by the pressure of the strong military lobby
in the United States. Kagan seems to affirm the view
that his favorite historian, the ancient Greek writer

Thucydides, might have taken of the "liberal and radical intellectuals" in Britain between the wars:

> Not for them the darker picture painted by a Thucydides of a human nature that remained largely the same over the centuries or of a human race that escaped chaos and barbarism by preserving with difficulty a thin layer of civilization by means of moderation and prudence based on a careful study of experience. (414)

Like his own. He worries that "the states with the greatest interest in peace and the greatest power to preserve it appear to be faltering in their willingness to pay the price in money and the risk of lives" (572). He aspires to be the Thucydides of our day, urging finally a strong military, a leader willing to use it, what he sees as a realistic facing up to global military responsibility, and the resolute eschewing of pacifism or social welfare. He uses the ancients to justify his sense of the immutability of humans' impulses to violence and aggression, not proving their universality, but through ancient example simply asserting it. The wars of the classical Greeks and Romans provide him with the foundation and the authority for his claims about the eternal inevitability of war. He uses classical antiquity to justify a contemporary politics of military expenditure, interventionism, and American imperial ambitions. His version of ancient history serves his political purposes, while distorting both history and the classics.

Victor Davis Hanson, farmer, classicist, and author

of *Fields without Dreams: Defending the Agrarian Idea,*
published by the Free Press in 1996, reminds the reader
of his agrarian ancestors, the ancient Greek Hesiod, and
the heroes of the comic poet Aristophanes. He is full of
rage at both bankers and urban intellectuals, briefly al-
lows that "feminist historians" may be right about
women's keeping the American farm alive, but writes
throughout as if he were completely untouched by the
notion, for example, that his constant use of "he,"
"men," and the like, to describe those who matter, ex-
cludes more than half the human race.[7]

The book is a pessimistic and self-righteous tirade
about the disappearing family farm in America, and a
call for agrarian resistance and policy reform to save the
farm. Hanson laments that "it is increasingly difficult
anymore to find a natural bedrock conservative. . . . His
political views [the agrarian's]—nearly exclusively Republican—are incidental to his conservatism. He expresses more a knee-jerk and blanket distaste for fashion, affluence, and leisure" (xx). The point of view in
this text varies. Hanson seems to be denouncing both
the wealthy right-winger and the left-wing urbanite in
the name of the agrarian, bedrock conservative; he himself has constructed a wall around his property and
threatens intruders like a member of a sectarian militia:
"No bank, no hoodlum, no broker will make it inside
that wall. . . . Knowledge of the principles of classical
fortification and siegecraft (poliorcetics) and ancient

Greek masonry is not entirely without use" (5). The most interesting aspect of his text arises from the sour and denunciatory tone in which it is written, and from the pleasure he clearly takes in being the cantankerous and surly heir of the ancient Greek citizen, an Aristophanic hero now victim of the bankers. He betrays real hatred of his workers, after announcing proudly: "As both Xenophon and Aristotle saw, there is little exploitation of one's fellow man in agriculture" (xvii). Having grown up in the San Joaquin Valley myself, and having worked in a cannery, I found this statement rather hard to take. Hanson's passage on the pickers of the grapes that become raisins, although employing the passive voice and a sort of indirect style that fails to announce whether these views are his own or those of "the agrarian," demonstrates what he means by "little exploitation." With heavy irony, he assigns the position of victim to "the right-wing self-made in farming," who apparently suffers more than his employees when they complain about laboring conditions on the farm:

> Not a few farmers have noticed that a missing roll of toilet-paper in their porto-toilets makes them clear and present dangers to the health of the entire Latino community, while the flannel-shirted, floppy-panted, hairnetted *vatos* in Fresno now gun down their own kindred. (39)

Hanson caricatures the reasoning of the "urban left-wing dupe," who "thinks nothing of the servitude of his

Hispanic gardener." His sympathies and the force of his argument clearly ally Hanson with this "right-wing self-made in farming." Solomonically, he announces the truth: "No grape picker can sustain himself in America as an American on farm-labor wages" (40). This is the "little exploitation" of the noble agrarian way of life: "You really cannot in a generation take a Third World native from the tropics and turn him into a bumbling suburbanite wrestling with his weed eater." "A vendetta over a woman? You stab deep and flee south" (40). There are many such passages, for example this, in praise of the non-American worker:

> Usually, when the picking starts, a carload of poor de-ranged whites, blacks, Mexican-Americans, or Hmong on welfare drive by the vineyard and say they are "directed" to work cutting grapes. So much for the local "human services" office's most recent pa-thetic efforts at "workfare." Apparently, grape season at least gets the lethal mass of slackers out of their of-fice for a day. Tattoos, guns, bandannas, knives, drug-induced malnourishment, wraparound sunglasses, tooth-gapped death stares, and Oakland Raider hats—the whole visual apparatus of the American criminal class that so frightens the rest of the world—do not amount to much when you're alone, crawling your way through two hundred vines in a row a quar-ter-mile long. (48)

In his view, most workers today are worthless, but Hanson's children are learning what they need to know by supervising the young, combative and cheating laborers he employs:

> Forget about the pretentious gifted program at the local school, which is neither gifted nor a program. It is far better for a child of ten to walk among swarthy, callused men of the knife and the bottle, checking their veracity with a cheap hand clicker. (47)

A swipe at education, a little anti-intellectualism, some uneasy irony, a little child labor, the master race ruling the swarthy masses with "little exploitation." If the agrarian way of life, the lineage from Hesiod, Aristophanes, Euripides, and Vergil, produces such virulence, can we really mourn its loss?

Hanson argues that democracy depends on the egalitarianism of the small farmer (although the worker is, obviously, excluded from this egalitarianism). He gloomily draws an analogy between the end of the Greek *polis* and our current situation. His conclusions resemble Kagan's; he calls for respect for physical work, reward for public service, the requirement of military duty, and "firmness" (274). Otherwise, decadence will lead to decline.

In a later book, *Who Killed Homer? The Demise of Classical Education and the Recovery of Greek Wisdom,* written with John Heath, Hanson polemically assumes the death of classical studies, although contemporary debates in fact suggest that what we now see is

a healthy disagreement over how to teach and inter-
pret antiquity, rather than a deathly absence of interpretations. The authors accuse all those they de-
nounce—including myself, all feminists, "British but-
lers," that is, classicists from Britain working in
America, and all those they rather loosely term "multiculturalists"—of assassinating "Homer," the poet who
stands for the classics, out of greed, careerism, and op-
portunism. The argument is that if we do not idealize
the Greeks, "think like Greeks," "match word with
deed" (47), and observe classical military discipline, as
they urge, if, on the contrary, we recognize that the
Greeks held slaves and were often misogynists, as well
as the inventors of democracy, the jury system, and
philosophy, we have participated in killing off the
fragile Greeks, and in murdering the great poet.

Heath and Hanson attribute the "killing" of Homer
to those who have failed to accept such "Greek" precepts
as the laconically expressed: "Human nature is constant
over time and place" (40), or "Private property and free
economic activity are immune from government coer-
cion and interference" (34). In fact, if "Homer" ever
lived (recent scholarship suggests that the epic poems at-
tributed to him are the work of a long oral tradition of
nameless bards), he would probably have died a natural
death by now. Is it necessary to "think like Greeks"
in order to study and teach classical civilization, as if
teaching and scholarship on historical subjects required

identification with the objects of that scholarship, as if students of Vichy France must of necessity "think like Pétainistes"? Historical study need not, probably ought not to, imply overt and conscious exhortations to return to the past, especially to a slave-owning, militarist, imperialist, often xenophobic, patriarchal culture like that of ancient Athens, much as we can learn from its study.

A typically melodramatic statement:

> All of us who teach the Greeks anywhere, according to our station, confront daily a set of realities that say the opposite of what we learn from the Greeks: obscure and safe publication, travel, title, pelf, narrowness, and university affiliation are everything, undergraduate teaching, matching word with deed, living like Greeks relatively nothing. At various times all of us weaken to honor what is killing us, only on other occasions to stiffen and embrace what still might save us. (xxi–xxii)

Phallic imagery aside, Hanson and Heath fail to recognize that there are other factors negatively affecting all historical and foreign language study in this country—the growing expense of education, allowing for less elective study of subjects such as ancient Greek, the need for students to establish credentials for future employment, the instrumentalizing of education and emphasis on technical training and vocational concentration, and a general tendency toward exclusive study of the present even in the humanities. A decline of student enrollment in ancient Greek cannot be laid solely at the feet of "feminists" and "multiculturalists." If enrollments in courses in the Greek and Roman classics have declined in recent years, it may rather be because there are too many scholars who believe, as Hanson and Heath do, that any realistic assessment of the contradictory and complex nature of Hellenic society damages the Greeks, so that teachers and professors must engage in an unrelenting campaign of promotion and idealization, perpetuating bygone illusions of a Greek paradise lost. This perspective is possibly unconvincing to today's students, who learn in other courses in the humanities to be critical of received traditions and of idealization.

The mere recognition that there are at least two genders, which barely surfaces in the work of Kagan and Hanson, is supplemented in the sexual theory of Camille Paglia, in *Sexual Personae*.[8] A romp of dazzling superficiality from the dawn of humankind to Emily Dickinson and beyond, featuring such pithy summaries of centuries of Roman history as "Republic to empire was like high classic to Hellenistic, unity to multiplicity," and "Eye plus orgy equals decadence"(130–31), this work, like that of Kagan, eschews linear history, relying on a notion of cycles, or, as she calls them, "phases," in its place. The Pythia, priestess of the Delphic oracle in classical Greece, is one of her "personae," the best example of which is Gracie Allen (47); Artemis leads her to Katherine Hepburn (80). This is a history of Western civilization that is merely the confirmation of sexual stereotypes, or, as she calls them, in a familiar allusion, "archetypes." In other words, she is a sort of Jungian sociobiologist, committed to an ahistorical notion of "nature" and gender difference, fueled by antifeminism and misogyny, exhibiting a disgust for the female body and an identification with "the beautiful boy."

> Nature is serpentine, a bed of tangled vines, creepers and crawlers, probing dumb fingers of fetid organic life which Wordsworth taught us to call pretty. Biologists speak of man's reptilian brain, the oldest part of our upper nervous system, killer survivor of the archaic era. I contend that the premenstrual woman incited to snappishness or rage is hearing signals from the reptilian brain. In her, man's latent perversity is manifest. All hell breaks loose, the hell of chthonian nature that modern humanism denies and represses. In every premenstrual woman struggling to govern her temper, sky-cult wars again with earth-cult. (12)

Paglia repeats the slanders of centuries of misogynists, who identify women with the natural, the irrational, the primitive, and the prehistoric. The book is self-congratulatory, the rant of someone assuming that she alone has the balls, the guts, the nerve to face the ugliness of reality, the brute facts of our animal nature: "The fatty female body is a sponge" (91). And the Greeks, of course, figure prominently in the narrative, validating it. For example:

What did survive, what did vanquish circumstance and
stamp its mind-set on Europe was Mycenaean warrior
culture, descending to us through Homer. The male
will-to-power: Mycenaeans from the south and Dori-
ans from the north would fuse to form Apollonian
Athens, from which came the Greco-Roman line of
Western history. (8)

While noting the Greek inheritance from Egypt, Paglia's
representation of classical Athenian culture relies on
well-worn conceptions of the Greek genius expressed
through a conflict between Nietzsche's Dionysiac and
Apollonian. Her sexual personae, her archetypes, are
eternal and essential: Gracie Allen *is* the Pythoness.

What do the Greeks owe to Egypt? Martin Bernal's
Black Athena has excited much reaction within the academy and without.[9] He argues that the field of classics
originated in the intellectual climate of the eighteenth
and nineteenth centuries, that early classicists were concerned to establish the European, Aryan origins of ancient Greek civilization, and thus denied the earlier
Greek acknowledgment of debts to Semitic Near Eastern and African, especially Egyptian, cultural neighbors.
He seeks in several volumes to demonstrate strong ties
among Asia, Africa, and Greece, going so far as to argue
for an Egyptian invasion and occupation of Greece in
the eighteenth century B.C.E. His ideas have been widely
debated; some scholars find persuasive his contentions

about the origins of the discipline of classics, many believe that classical scholarship has already long recognized Greece's debt to its neighbors in Asia and Africa,
and few are persuaded by his etymologies and claims for
an Egyptian occupation of mainland Greece. Yet his
work has had a salutary effect on the field, leading classicists to look critically at the scholarly assumptions at
the beginnings of their field, and to emphasize the in-
terdependence and interrelations of the ancient Aegean
cultures at the expense of what was once thought to be
a Greek "miracle," the almost magical emergence of a
fully evolved Greek culture uncontaminated by neighboring Asia and Africa.

The classicist Mary Lefkowitz, professor of humanities at Wellesley College, has been welcomed in the
public domain as the most prominent and vocal an-
tagonist of Bernal. In her critique of Bernal, *Not Out
of Africa,* a publication funded by the Olin Foundation, aligning Bernal with all Afrocentrists, she cites
George G. M. James, W. E. B. DuBois, and Marcus
Garvey, as well as contemporary Afrocentrists like
Leonard Jeffries and Tony Martin, as if there were no
distinctions among them, no other points of view on
the question of Afrocentrism among African-American historians, intellectuals, and academics. Why is
she so bent on denouncing the Afrocentrists, especially those who claim primacy for African culture,
and its historical priority over Hellenic civilization?

She justifies her passion in part through an argument about cultural superiority, sliding from the idea of priority or originality to supremacy, and in effect neglecting Bernal's arguments about classicists' disregard of ancient Semitic and Near Eastern cultures in favor of an exclusive denunciation of Afrocentrism.

In fact, some Afrocentric texts are the work of popular writers, sometimes autodidacts with restricted access to scholarly training and resources. Lefkowitz claims that in their work the Greeks are being maligned and accused of theft, and her identification with the Greeks themselves seems to motivate her to respond with a certain rage. She is concerned to discredit all Afrocentrists, some of whom point to a real ignorance of and disregard for African history in American universities. Certainly this is a matter of some significance, worth emphasizing. There is in fact a kind of censorship by exclusion. A huge continent, Africa, which has a long history, is poorly represented in terms of investment in research and curriculum in American universities.

Lefkowitz is most concerned about the displacement of the classics from the center of the curriculum, although this is an imaginary centrality, as Larry Levine points out in *The Opening of the American Mind*:[10]

> [Robert] Hutchins's nostalgia for an education that never, or at best rarely, existed in the United States, has become a central part of the critique of the American university that exists in our own day. We keep hearing

45

romantic calls for the "restoration" of the classical tradition in a Great Books version that is itself a relatively
recent invention. (52)

The Western Civ curriculum, portrayed by some critics
of the university in our time as apolitical and of ex-
tremely long duration, was in fact neither. It was a
twentieth-century phenomenon which had its origins
in a wartime government initiative, and its heyday
lasted for scarcely fifty years. (73)

. . . [T]he canonical inevitably is affected by cultural circumstances and transformations as we have seen. The
rise of industrial America finally led to the demise of
the classical curriculum and the adoption of the elective
system; World War I promoted a sense of Western civilization; World War II and the Cold War heightened
the sense of Americanness and a concern with things
American. The rise of the Third World, the decline of
European hegemony, the civil rights and women's
movements, and the entry of new ethnic and racial mi-
norities into the academic world as both students and
teachers during the past several decades have promoted
significant cultural and canonical changes which numerous colleagues have rejected as somehow uniquely
political—overly tainted by the secular and the imme-
diate rather than the sacred and the timeless, which is
the way they have imagined canons to be. (99–100)

Fears about the displacement of the classics from the
center of the curriculum, and about distraction from the
study of the supposed origins of our civilization have

been voiced from early on in the evolution of the American educational system:

> In 1820 the Western Review warned Transylvania University in Kentucky that if Latin and Greek should ever cease to be taught in our universities, and the study of Cicero, Demosthenes, Homer, and Virgil thought unnecessary, "we should regard mankind as fast sinking into absolute barbarism, and the gloom of mental darkness as likely to increase until it should become universal." (38–39)

To match a story Lefkowitz tells, and later repeats in *Black Athena Revisited,* of a deluded student who, led astray by an Afrocentric professor, thought Socrates was black, I offer this one. I teach in an undergraduate sequence called "The Making of the Modern World" that is meant to be a history of the world, not just Europe and the Americas, not just Western civilization. My students in this course come from families of African, Asian, Indian subcontinental, Pacific Island, Native American, Latin American, and European origins. Once when I was being briefed on the sequence, of which I teach the ancient history term—ancient Mesopotamia, Israel, Egypt, Greece, India, and China (a prejudicial selection no doubt)—someone reported to me that some students had come to the faculty asking that more attention be paid to African history in the next course, the Roman and medieval section of the two-year cycle. This person rolled her eyes in exasperation while recounting this episode, taking for granted that I would share her impatience and irritation at such a request. The assumption is that Africa has no history, or that if it does, it cannot possibly rank among the big three continents, the "strong" cultures of the world.

Lefkowitz's assault on Afrocentrism must be read in the context of this environment, in which a Western civilization curriculum, eternally classical, is mourned by many, and in which an African-American studies department at Harvard has attracted some of the most distinguished and influential intellectuals in America today.

Classical studies are and should be part of historical study; the ancient Greeks and Romans are part of our heritage, and were thought, with ancient Israel, to constitute our origins by generations of Western intellectuals. But they are only part of the story. We need to understand our place in global history, America's cultural debts to Africa, Latin America, Asia, the Indian subcontinent, the Pacific Islands, to all those parts of the world that have sent slaves or indentured workers or immigrants to America, to all those peoples who have engaged and will continue to engage in various forms of economic and cultural exchange with North America, to those parts of the world that have been visited or invaded or exploited by Americans, areas that have influenced American culture and will have increasing contact with the United States. One can no longer claim that Hebraic and classical Greek civilizations are the sole origins of a pristine Western culture; we owe to them only part of what we are. And national identity, the understanding Western nation-states have of themselves, is only part of what students who live in the global twenty-first century need to know.

The attack on Afrocentrism seems to me to be an assault on a straw man. There are errors in some Afrocentric texts, pointed out scrupulously by Lefkowitz. But she is either complicit with or the instrument of a policy that seeks to focus all attention on these errors, and thus to direct attention away from much else that is happening in American universities, including a necessary attention to other histories besides those of ancient Greece. Lefkowitz's outrage and insistence on denouncing inaccuracies draw attention away from the real need in American universities to teach differently, to include the histories of Africa, for example, in introductory civilization courses, rather than to continue teaching only the European heritage in Western civilization courses. Lefkowitz uses allusions to the Holocaust, the Germans' genocidal attempt to annihilate the Jews, to whip up a certain hysteria about her ideas of truth:

> Academics ought to have seen right from the start that this "new historicism" has some serious shortcomings. But in fact most of us are just beginning to emerge from the fog far enough to see where history-without-facts

can lead us, which is right back to fictive history of the kind developed to serve the Third Reich. It is not coincidental that ours is the era not just of Holocaust denial but of denial that the ancient Greeks were ancient Greeks and creators of their own intellectual heritage.[11]

As if Bernal were a "new historicist," as if myth were not part of history, fictions not part of history, history not the writing of texts, as if facts existed autonomously, without interpretation and presentation and selection, as if the ancient Greeks miraculously conjured themselves up from nothing.

There are illogical moments in Lefkowitz's own arguments. For example:

Most ironically, by claiming as African a myth that is fundamentally European, the Afrocentrists make Africa the source of the culture that they blame for their own troubles. (156)

Yet if some Africans in the early modern period were enslaved by Europeans, and transported to the Americas as slaves, and if Africa was colonized, divided up, and exploited by European states in the modern period, then these are indeed some of the European "troubles" of Africa, not ultimately the responsibility of Africans themselves. It seems to me that some classicists' elision of a cultural debt owed to Egypt by the ancient Greeks is quite consistent with such brutality and exploitation.

Lefkowitz goes through an elaborate denunciation of

Shelley Haley, one of very few African American classicists, claiming that what has always been thought about Cleopatra, that she was a "white" Macedonian, must be the case, when Lefkowitz's own argument reveals clearly that *we don't know*:

> Because the normal practice of ancient writers was to make as much as possible out of any anomaly or scandal, such as a love affair with or marriage to a foreigner, we can also presume that Cleopatra's grandmother and mother were Greek, because no ancient writer comments on them. Although the ancients were in general without color prejudice, they were sensitive to differences in appearance, background, and in language. They called foreigners *barbaroi* because what they said did not make sense—at least to Greek ears. So it is more likely that Cleopatra's grandmother was a Greek, and not a slave, because that would be the most unremarkable possible identity. Admittedly that is an argument from silence, but that is the only kind of argument we can make without specific factual information. (45)

In other words, we don't *know* who Cleopatra's grandmother was. She may very well have been an Egyptian, an African. Lefkowitz goes to great lengths, here and elsewhere, to show that North Africans and Egyptians are not "really" African. Discussing an argument by Yosef A. A. ben-Jochannan, who says that St. Augustine, his mother Monnica, and Tertullian, the early church father, among others, were "indigenous Africans," she says evidence suggests "that they were actually Carthaginian or Roman, rather than African in the modern sense of the word" (32). Here Lefkowitz seems to be suggesting that "African" can only mean "negro"/"black African"/ "sub-Saharan African." And that Augustine, of course, wasn't one of "them"; her argument is inescapably racist. In my opinion, African, in the modern and all other senses, means from Africa; no one denies that Augustine was born in Thagaste, now in Algeria, now in North Africa. How is this not Africa, not indigenous, not African?

In their edited book *Black Athena Revisited,* Mary Lefkowitz and Guy MacLean Rogers again attack Martin Bernal, including an essay bolstered by statistics asking the question, "Who were the ancient Egyptians?" The authors conclude:

> Attempts to force the Egyptians into either a "black" or a "white" category have no biological justification. Our data show not only that Egypt clearly had biological ties both to the north and to the south, but that it was intermediate between populations of the east and the west, and that Egypt was basically Egyptian from the Neolithic right on up to historic times.[12]

They quite rightly argue that race is not a useful concept for dealing with the realities of Egypt, ancient and modern. The very desire to establish racially pure categories itself arouses suspicions of racism. In the context of the volume attacking Bernal's work, however, the essay buttresses arguments like Lefkowitz's that Egypt and ancient Carthage are somehow mysteriously not *in Africa,* not African, when the whole point is that they are in fact in Africa. Attempting to keep Egypt separate from the rest of the continent of Africa does smack of racism and of an attempt to establish an uncontaminated racial pedigree for intellectual forebears. In Lefkowitz's view, St. Augustine couldn't be an African, he must be a Carthaginian, that is, a Semite or a Roman, that is, a "Caucasian," even though he was born in Africa.

In *The Black Atlantic,* Paul Gilroy offers arguments that help explain the interest of many people who belong to the African diaspora in Afrocentrist histories. Like Lefkowitz, he is critical of those who argue for racial purity as a basis for racial solidarity against racism, yet he contextualizes Afrocentrism as a political and rhetorical strategy in a world where racism persists:

> The idea of tradition gets understandably invoked to underscore the historical continuities, subcultural conversations, intertextual and intercultural cross-fertilisations which make the notion of a distinctive and self-conscious black culture appear plausible. This usage is important and inescapable because racisms work insidiously and consistently to deny both historicity and cultural integrity to the artistic and cultural fruits of black life.[13]

It is precisely this nuanced, historical reading of Afrocentricity that Lefkowitz's volumes lack. Her work mounts a rhetorically violent and phobic defense against the possibility that the classics will be displaced from the imaginary center of an eternal and correct canon, and that her truth concerning the Greeks' "creation" of their own culture will be eroded, as if any society invents itself out of whole cloth, sealed off from surrounding cultures and their influences.

The following are some features of the family resemblance shared to varying degrees by the writers discussed above, who have published work about the ancient world for a popular audience:

There is a fascination and a nostalgia for war.

There is a commitment to bolstering the military and the small family farm, and an idealization of the (male) citizen-farmer-soldier.

Democracy is feared as mob rule, unless accompanied by strong leaders and a censored education.

History is narrative history, events recounted as if they themselves had meaning and needed no interpretation, as if they were all equivalent, as if there were no epochal differences.

Facts are isolated from the totalities in which they are imbedded, and the rhetoric of their presentation is ignored.

There is a belief in the human condition, in human

nature, which is never historicized, but seen as absolute and enduring.

This human condition is described without consideration of such features as gender difference, and militarism and conservatism are assumed to be appropriate to the universal subject, the white European male.

Ancient Greece is fetishized and idolized as the origin of Western civilization, which is in turn considered to be the single source of our contemporary culture.

3

Aliens

In *Fields without Dreams: Defending the Agrarian Idea,* discussed in the preceding chapter, Victor Davis Hanson writes of the ideal citizen whose characteristics he traces back to ancient Greece:

> With Hesiod's world begins the entire notion of agrarianism that was soon to become the foundation of the Greek city-state, and later to be enshrined in the West as the exemplar of a democratic society: a culture of small, independent yeomen on the land, who make their own laws, fight their own battles, and create a community of tough like-minded individuals.[14]

His description of life on a raisin farm in the Central Valley of California abounds with tough, independent yeoman talk like this:

> I think most [Mexican] laborers, if not killed by one another, injured, or jailed, stay up north to spawn an impoverished but enormous family that inevitably plugs into the declining social services of an exhausted state. Without money an illegal immigrant can still strut in town if, cometlike, he has attached to his rear a long winding tail of a second litter of offspring. (41)

This book abounds in xenophobia and contempt. Such is the link made, on the best-seller list and elsewhere, between ancient Greece, its democratic citizenry, and questions of citizenship and immigration in North America today. In California we have recently seen referenda demanding that English only be used in all public transactions, that bilingual education be abolished, that immigrants be denied social services, and arguments that immigration from Latin America be abolished entirely. And the success of some of these enterprises owes something to scholarly claims about the nature of the Western heritage and of American democracy.

Like Victor Hanson, Donald Kagan, Mary Lefkowitz, Allan Bloom, and William Bennett also mine classical antiquity for lessons concerning our political system and the need to protect it from immigrants of the wrong sort, from sloppy Afrocentric thought, and from a lack of virtue, defined in part as obedience to leaders like Kagan's Pericles and his analogue in the present, Henry Kissinger. As I have argued—these thinkers, and I include Camille Paglia among them—share, with various exceptions and differences, certain opinions. They believe in an unchanging, fixed "human nature," and enjoy discovering evidence of the eternal greed and selfishness of people in all historical periods and locations. They congratulate themselves on their tough-mindedness and chastise others for sentimentality and for an interested and political manipulation of the past. They argue for "peace through strength," for strong leaders and militant militarism. Most tend to ignore the existence of women. Their Greeks are tailored to fit their political criteria.

In other intellectual distortions, conservative political thinkers misrepresent ancient Greek democracy. Some, like Allan Bloom, condemn it as mob rule. Others claim that Athenian democracy worked as well as it did primarily because of the homogeneity of the citizen population of ancient Athens. In such campaigns as the English-only effort, like-minded politicians suggest that American democracy works best with citizens of the same kind. While ignoring the primacy of the indigenous population of the United States, they echo the ancient Athenians' mythology concerning autochthonous birth from the soil of the city itself, after Hephaistos's attempted rape of the goddess Athena. In fact, Athenians used the myth of autochthony as a rule to exclude newcomers, foreigners, and slaves from citizenship and from ownership of the city's land, but on rare occasions, there were citizens admitted to the Greek state who had formerly been slaves, born in other Greek cities or elsewhere in the Mediterranean world. Exceptionally, citizenship was awarded, for example, to citizens of allied cities and even to slaves who fought bravely in battle, in defense of Athens.

Our contemporaries, seeking deliberately to justify their own politics through reference to the ancient

Greeks, emphasizing the homogeneity of ancient city-states, exaggerate the Greeks' reliance on individual leaders. Donald Kagan, discussed earlier, author of *Pericles of Athens and the Birth of Democracy,* published by the Free Press, praises the ancient Greek aristocrat Pericles for masterful guidance of his state, and in an implicit argument for strong leadership suggests that it was only with Pericles at the helm that the Athenian democracy functioned successfully, inevitably to collapse after his death.[15] Yet, as Kagan himself acknowledges, through the institution called ostracism the citizens of Athens provided systematically for a way to rid the state of anyone who became too powerful and threatened domination or incipient tyranny in the city.

Some contemporary writers obscure the radical, experimental, and contradictory nature of Athenian democracy in the fifth century B.C.E. Kagan, although writing the kind of history that involves "just the facts," does engage in the occasional editorial comment meant to illuminate our current situation. For example:

> equality before the law, not equality of possession, was the only form of the principle compatible with prosperity, freedom, and security. For the Athenians, therefore, social justice did not mean economic leveling. The Athenian democrat demanded equality of opportunity, a "career open to talents." But he also believed that excellence and superior ability should be rewarded. (272)

Kagan's is an anachronistic projection of contemporary notions of "equal opportunity" on a radically different set of social arrangements, apparently inserted lest we imagine the exemplary Athenians to have been communists, or "economic levelers."

The boundaries of the citizen population were not controlled as absolutely as some suggest, and there was a marked wariness about inherited aristocratic privilege among politicians. Athens as a democracy was also committed in principle to the distribution of its own wealth, tribute, taxes, and war booty to the citizens of Athens and to the beautification of its public spaces, its marketplaces and temples.

Nonetheless, there were ways in which the ideal citizen, especially in theory, *did* share the characteristics named by Hanson and yearned for nostalgically by many today. The ideal Athenian citizen *was* imagined by the ancestors of these thinkers as autochthonous, as born from the soil of the city and therefore part of the landscape for millenia, as a brother of his fellow-citizens going back for generations, as forged into a phalanx by required military service. Such beliefs produced a citizenry that was sometimes xenophobic and often misogynist. The philosopher Aristotle, a resident of Athens for part of his life, although never an Athenian citizen, said: "A citizen pure and simple is defined by nothing else so much as by the right to participate in judicial functions and in office" (*Politics* 1275a).[16] That is to say, resident aliens, slaves, and women were not citizens.

The definitions of a good citizen differed. The Athenian citizen Plato, often a man of atypical opinion, wrote that a citizen is a child and servant of the laws, must control his passions, must not be greedy of riches, nor praised until dead, must not lead an idle life, nor practice trade or handicrafts, and must not take part in performances of comedy:

> "We shall enjoin that such representations be left to slaves or hired aliens, and that they receive no serious consideration whatsoever." (*Laws* 816e)[17]

In his discussion about the poets in the *Republic,* Plato argued that much poetry is harmful to the education of the good citizen:

> "We must begin, then, it seems, by a censorship over our story-makers, and what they do well we must pass and what not, reject. And the stories on the accepted list we will induce nurses and mothers to tell to the children and so shape their souls by these stories far rather than their bodies by their hands. But most of the stories they now tell we must reject." (377bc)

He mentioned, without specifying the details, the story of the castration of the god Ouranos by his son Kronos, among other scandalous myths about the gods: "Even if they were true I should not think that they ought to be thus lightly told to thoughtless young persons"

(377e–378a). Like William Bennett, who bowdlerizes Greek myth and history for his best-selling book of virtuous stories, Plato argued, against the tradition of Greek culture, and with little apparent success, for the expurgation of the violent or erotic episodes in the mythological tradition.

In the philosopher's view, the good citizen stayed put. Plato's teacher Socrates, when given a choice between exile and hemlock, chose execution by the citizens of Athens, having never left Athens except for his military service. Plato wrote concerning Socrates's rootedness in Athens:

> "You would not have been so exceptionally reluctant to cross the borders of your country if you had not been exceptionally attached to it. You have never left the city to attend a festival or for any other purpose, except on some military expedition. You have never traveled abroad as other people do, and you have never felt the impulse to acquaint yourself with another country or constitution." (*Crito* 52b)

> "You could not have absented yourself from the city less if you had been lame or blind or decrepit in some other way." (53a)

The good citizen in this early political theory was male, the heir of many generations of citizens themselves descended from the gods and from Attica, the land of Athens itself, neither an artisan nor a worker, raised on virtuous stories or none at all, and fixed, immobile, rarely traveling except as a soldier, never migrating, and choosing execution over exile.

Athenians prided themselves on descent from the land of Athens herself, and their celebration of purity and autochthony is echoed in American xenophobia and anti-immigrationist policies such as the English-only referenda. The Athenians accused residents of other Greek cities of mixed, impure tongues and of descent from barbarians, from Kadmos, Danaos, Pelops, or Egypt. In one of Plato's dialogues the speaker says: "we are pure Hellenes, uncontaminated by any foreign element, and therefore the hatred of the foreigner has passed unadulterated into the lifeblood of the city" (*Menexenus* 245d). This dialogue, an imaginary funeral oration to be pronounced for the Athenian dead, is said to have been composed by the non-Athenian Aspasia, but her rhetoric resembles that of many such orations. And if Plato was mocking such chauvinism, we find it elsewhere in boasts that claim the Athenians' superiority to the inhabitants of other Greek cities. Such citizens were said to live in added-on rooms, to be like adopted children. Only the Athenians had an unmixed origin, born from the very earth of their territory Attica, thereafter a purely masculine descent from Hephaistos and Erichthonios. Only the Athenians never emigrated (Herodotos 7.161); they traced their history straight back, without deviation or passage elsewhere, to the god's insemination of the earth. Their city and its citizens were homogeneous, unmixed, and spoke the purest Attic Greek. And the claim was that the city functions best with such citizens, who understand themselves to be a single family, formed of identical households, without strife because composed of "sons of the same mother" (Plato, *Republic* 3.414e). Aristotle said in the *Politics* (4.1295b25–29): "But surely the ideal of the state is to consist as much as possible of persons that are equal and alike." This model of government—the celebration of purity, homogeneity, stasis, and immobility—is taken up, ironically, by Americans whose ancestors were immigrants, later "naturalized," some of whose forebears exterminated those with a much greater claim to autochthony than theirs, and who use it to justify pseudo-democratic, in fact oligarchic nationalism and what are sometimes called family values, that is, patriarchal dominance in the heterosexual nuclear family.

In France, too, ancient history has at certain moments served the right. Neo-Fascists have used a particular reading of the ancient Greek city-state to argue for xenophobia and the exclusion of immigrants from political rights. A right-wing legislator in the National Assembly read into the record a long discourse about autochthony, celebrating the rootedness of the ancient Athenians in their own land, and extended this to argue for the right-wing slogan, "France for the French." The Neo-Fascists still want to maintain France as a Catholic nation, founded by the Christian Clovis, while the "others," including Arabs, Muslims, and Jews, once called *métèques,* like "metics," resident aliens in the ancient Greek city, would be excluded from the homogeneous body politic.

The portrait of the good citizen drawn by Plato and Aristotle has been taken up again by those relying on antiquity to justify their political program in the present, one celebrating heterosexuality, male domination, homogeneity, private property rights, and isolationism, while refusing immigration, nomadism, and internationalism. As a prelude to my discussion of what is suppressed in their accounts of the Greeks, in sex, politics, and religion, I propose another genealogy that also looks back to antiquity, but would descend from the ancient Greek poet Sappho. Sappho will stand here for a whole strain of Greek antiquity rarely represented in the texts which I find so ahistorical and reductive. There are many strands in the Greek tradition, some that share characteristics very different from those to which the right appeals, authors who value pleasure, write from outside Athens, advocate the mixture of peoples, and question the institution of slavery, others who relativize the aristocratic, antidemocratic tradition, writers and thinkers like Gorgias, Herodotus, the sophists, Protagoras, Antiphon, and others. I invoke Sappho as an example to recall to cultural memory not just her work, but also the curious and peripatetic Herodotus, who wrote about the Greeks' neighbors, from the Scythians to the Egyptians, and decenters for the modern reader a Greek world focused only on Athens. She must also recall for us all those poets who valued pleasure and eros, who themselves read Sappho, poets like Aeschylus and Pindar, who sang songs of praise for Sicilian victors in the Olympian and other games. And she represents here, for the sake of brevity, all those Greek artists who learned from neighboring cultures, imitating and transforming their art, and indeed all the contradictory intricacy to be found even at the heart of the most canonical literary and cultural texts of classical Athens itself.

Sappho was first of all a woman, therefore not eligible for citizenship in Aristotle's and Plato's terms. She might have given birth to a citizen son if his father were a citizen, but in classical Athens itself she could never have been a citizen within Aristotle's definition, since she could never have exercised any judicial functions nor served in any political office. Furthermore, Sappho was a Lesbian, a resident of the island of Lesbos, situated far from the Greek mainland, near Lydia on the coast of Asia, and susceptible to aristocratic luxuriousness and Asiatic ways despised by the Athenian political theorists. Plato exiled the "Lydian," or Asiatic mode of poetry from his republic (*Republic* 398e). Sappho's family may have had roots in Asia. Her poems did not seek to instill virtue, or to communicate the noblest stories about the gods, as Plato would have wished. They did not encourage women to be good wives, nor to reproduce citizens for the city. Sappho's fragment 16 reads:

Some say an army of horsemen, others
say foot-soldiers, still others, a fleet,
is the fairest thing on the dark earth:
I say it is whatever one loves.

Everyone can understand this—
consider that Helen, far surpassing
the beauty of mortals, leaving behind
the best man of all,

sailed away to Troy. She had no
memory of her child or dear parents,
since she was led astray
[by Kypris] . . .

*
     . . . lightly
. . . reminding me now of Anaktoria
being gone,

I would rather see her lovely step
and the radiant sparkle of her face
than all the war-chariots in Lydia
and soldiers battling in shining bronze.[18]

This broken, fragmentarily preserved poem, consciously and deliberately or not, sets itself against the militarist Homeric tradition, and the reinterpretation of those values evolving in city-states like Athens, in which would develop the ideal citizen, and where the good citizen woman, with her fertile body metaphorically linked to the city's fields, would produce a crop of sons for the city's military forces.

First of all, Sappho turns away from the army, the navy, and the cavalry, those armed forces dear to the Greek political thinkers, and to such contemporary writers as Donald Kagan and Victor Davis Hanson. She does not find the sight of horsemen, ships, and foot soldiers to be as universally beautiful as "whatsoever one loves." And as proof she adduces the markedly unvirtuous Helen of Troy, seen later as the ruiner of cities, and feared and despised by the chorus of the citizen tragedian Aeschylus. In offering her as an example, Sappho seems almost to celebrate Helen, who disregarded family values, abandoning husband and child, following her lover, the one whom she loved, perhaps urged on by the goddess of eros Aphrodite. Sappho's use of Helen, a figure from the Homeric narrative of the Trojan War, appears scandalous in a world rapidly concurring on a consensus that Helen was a monster. Sappho's contemporary Alcaeus, for example, sang:

As the story goes, because of evil deeds bitter grief came once to Priam and his sons from you, Helen, and Zeus destroyed holy Ilium with fire. (fr. 42)

. . . crazed by the Trojan man, the deceiver of his host, she [Helen] accompanied him over the sea in his ship, leaving in her home her child [desolate?] and her husband's bed. . . . many of [Paris's] brothers [the dark

earth?] holds, laid low on the Trojans' plain for that
woman's sake. . . . (fr. 283)

For Alcaeus, who elsewhere celebrated the ship of state,
and its soldier's weaponry, Helen was a mad, dangerous
destroyer who annihilated Troy, the mythical citadel of
the past. In so doing she also betrayed the values of the
incipient city-state. For Sappho, she is the exemplar of
one who follows her desire, and in remembering Helen
the poet is reminded of her own object of desire, Anaktoria, whom Sappho prefers over chariots and infantry.

Sappho is an ancestor of another sort, a counter to
the patriarchal, male-centered, philosophical city imagined by Plato and Aristotle and some of their heirs,
thinkers of the present day. She refuses the political values of the city, she desires women and does not celebrate
either their reproductive power or their potential con-
tribution to the city's armies and fleet. She looks toward
Asia rather than toward the mainland of Greece. She
writes in another fragment of a woman now in Sardis, in
Asia Minor, "standing out among Lydian women." She
seems to make no distinction between the inhabitants of
Lesbos and this woman in Sardis, and like Herodotus
she writes of a diverse, cosmopolitan Mediterranean
universe. Her brother traveled to Egypt, one of those
merchants, it is thought, who strengthened the ties between Africa and the Greek islands, migrating, trading,
and carrying goods and culture to and from the Asians,

Africans, and Europeans, themselves hybrid and shaped by all three of these cultures.

And unlike Socrates, who never moved except to fight in Athens's army, Sappho herself seems to have chosen exile and travel over an identity fixed in her native soil. The Parian marble, two fragments of a marble stele from the island of Paros incised in 264 B.C.E., mentions a journey taken by the poet. This report of Sappho's travel, which must have occurred between 605 and 591 B.C.E., was made long after the event, but records a persistent tradition. The Roman Cicero mentions a statue of Sappho that stood in the town hall of Syracuse, in Sicily, until it was stolen. Because of political struggles in her city of Mytilene, and the temporary victory of the opposition party, Sappho was said to have embarked on this very long voyage, from the eastern edge of the Mediterranean, closest to Asia, to Sicily in the west. Like her brother, she was a migrant, refusing the nativist immobility and fixity of the Athenian citizen Socrates.

Needless to say, the Lesbian Sappho is not mentioned among the inspiring stories in the *Book of Virtues* collected by William Bennett, nor in Donald Kagan's accounts of the Greeks and their wars, nor in Victor Hanson's disgruntled tracing of his own descent from the Greeks through Hesiod and Aristophanes. She does figure in the chaotic and self-indulgent narrative of Camille Paglia, who might seem to perceive herself as the culmination of Western civilization. Paglia mentions Sappho several times, as in this passage:

> Western love has been ambivalent from the start. As early as Sappho (600 B.C.) or even earlier in the epic legend of Helen of Troy, art records the push and pull of attraction and hostility in that perverse fascination we call love. There is a magnetics of eroticism in the west, due to the hardness of western personality.[19]

Although Paglia *is* interested in women, in other ways her work resembles that of Kagan, Hanson, Bennett, et al. Here we see an essentializing description of personality qualified as "Western," hermetically sealed off from the "Eastern," but still ahistorical and absolute, along with the emphasis on individuals that fails to recognize other features of human history such as economic and social relations with "Eastern" civilizations. Paglia's history is an erasure of historical difference.

If we are interested in tracing a genealogy to counter an ahistorical filiation that celebrates a homogenized, white, European ancestry derived from Greek models, that sets itself against immigration as soon as European immigration to the United States has concluded, that condemns Asian, Pacific, African, and Latin American immigration in the perjured name of democracy, then I would set Sappho and other Greek thinkers like her against antiquarianism and the representations of the Greeks as monolithically male, Aryan, militarist, agrarian, and conservative. Let her stand with other Greek figures for something other than autochthony, a racialized fantasy of purity, a closed male citizen body, the subordination of women and slaves, the restriction of women to reproduction, and citizen immobility and stability. Her work, still very Greek, points in another, more daedalic direction—toward a polymorphous eroticism, toward pleasure and poetry, toward same-sex love, devotion, memory, toward hybridity, Asian, African, and European beginnings, toward nomadism and wandering and migration and the fertilization of one culture by another.

4

Sex

We have seen what "their Greeks" look like. I would argue for Sappho as a different beginning point for understanding the disparate and abundant histories of ancient Greek societies. And I want to look here at some examples of ancient Greek sex, politics, and religion, to locate signs of a greater density and ambiguity in ancient culture, to find the unfamiliar and the strange, those Greeks like the Asian and nomadic Herodotus, the wandering sophists, and poets like Sappho, often left out of work by the contemporary writers I've discussed.

Even in contemporary, allegedly secular, multicultural American society, we see the persistence of underlying religious assumptions about human sexuality, notions of shame, and the call both to police sexual behavior and to deny sexual education to the young. Reading the ancient Greeks provides a perspective on our own practices, and on our heritage, putting it into history. Our ideas about sexuality are not natural or inevitable; they are the legacy of a particular historical development, always in the process of change. Our ancestors the Greeks had very different ideas about bodies from ours, about what people should and did do with them, and about the relationship of their gods to sexuality.

"Sexuality" as a category, in the social scientific sense, as an object for Kinsey-like research, may not even be historically appropriate to the study of Greek society; rather, what we call sex was for the Greeks inseparable from worship of the gods, from ideas about origins and the relationship between human beings and their deities, from the duties of the citizen, and from ideas about philosophical knowledge.

The Greeks did have images of familial devotion, especially on funerary monuments, where husbands and wives left tender inscriptions remembering one another and their children. But they also had ideas about this part of human existence, the family, unlike our own, as well as different ideas about women's desire, about homoeroticism, and about obscenity. For example, sex between married partners was to some extent understood as an obligation, performed in order to guarantee the future and survival of household, family, and city. Husbands were required by law to have sex with their wives a certain number of times per month. Herodotus tells a story about an Athenian tyrant who failed to fulfill his duties:

After the recovery of his tyranny . . . Peisistratos married Megacles' daughter, as he had agreed to do; but because of a story that Megacles' family, the Alkmaionidai, had a curse upon it, and because he already had grown-up sons of his own, he did not want children from his new wife, and to prevent her from having any he had sex with her in a way contrary to custom. For a time his wife concealed these things, but later—perhaps in answer to a question—she told her mother, and her mother told her husband, who was so angry at the slight upon himself and his daughter, that he made up his quarrel with his political enemies. Learning of these doings, Peisistratos decided to leave the country. (Herodotus, *Histories* 1.61)

Marital sexual intercourse, with its potential for procreation, is conceived of here as a duty to be carried out by a husband with his wife; it is an obligation that touches the whole of an extended family, and crucially involves issues of dynastic honor.

In addition to such forms of marital responsibility, in the ancient Greek city relationships of exploitation and domination were often expressed sexually. Citizen men legally, politically, socially, and sexually dominated women, male and female slaves, and boys. Some scholars argue that the Athenian citizen, male and free, was understood to be the penetrator, the dominant partner in sexual relations, and that all others were conceived of as passive recipients, as "the penetrated." Sexual relations thus reinforced the hierarchies of power and status in the ancient city-state.

Exploring the Greeks' ways of organizing the domain of sexual life might lead us to question our own society's familiar vocabulary about such matters, polemics that naturalize feminine modesty and chastity, homophobia, and discrimination against gays and lesbians. Our exploration might make us suspicious of readings of ancient Greek society that ignore alternatives to such practices. The *Homeric Hymn to Aphrodite,* for example, an early song composed in praise of the Greek goddess called Venus by the Romans, points to the multiplicity of Greek ideas about sex, and the difference between these ideas and more modern ones. In this song the poet describes the passage of the goddess Aphrodite through the mountains near Troy. As she moves by, collecting a band of animals that accompanies her, the desire for coupling seizes them, and they mate on the mountainside:

> . . . *along with her, fawning, dashed gray wolves*
> *and lions with gleaming eyes and bears and swift leopards,*
> *ever hungry for deer. And when she saw them, she was*
> *delighted*
> *in her heart and placed longing in their breasts,*
> *so that they lay together in pairs along the shady glens.*[20]

This goddess, she who puts sexual passion into all things, animals and human, brings desire into the world; scholars have connected her to the Near Eastern goddesses of fertility, Ishtar and Astarte. The poet describes Aphrodite as herself subject to Eros, inflicted by Zeus with desire for Anchises, one of the fifty sons of King Priam of Troy. She appears to Anchises on the mountain:

*She was clothed in a robe more brilliant than gleaming fire
and wore spiral bracelets and shining earrings,
while round her tender neck there were beautiful necklaces,
lovely, golden and of intricate design. Like the moon's
was the radiance round her soft breasts, a wonder to the eye.*
(86–90)

The prince returns her passion; the poet sings of how Anchises disrobes the goddess for the act of love:

*smile-loving Aphrodite,
turning her face away, with beautiful eyes downcast, went
    coyly
to the well-made bed, which was already laid
with soft coverings for its lord.
On it were skins of bears and deep-roaring lions,
which he himself had killed on the high mountains.
And when they climbed onto the well-wrought bed,
first Anchises took off the bright jewels from her body,
brooches, spiral bracelets, earrings and necklaces,
and loosed her girdle, and her brilliant garments
he stripped off and laid upon a silver studded seat.
Then by the will of the gods and destiny he, a mortal,
lay beside an immortal, not knowing what he did.* (161–67)

This cult song, composed and performed as part of the worship of the goddess Aphrodite, reveals a range of religious beliefs and practices, an acceptance and celebration of desire and sensuality, of divine female desire, very different from notions of divinity in Judaic and Christian monotheisms. Although we cannot know the relationship between this scene of divine love and actual human behavior in the Greek world, it demonstrates an acceptance of erotic passion atypical of some contemporary religious sentiment. Christians would probably find it difficult to imagine their divinity in such circumstances.

The Greeks conceived of the goddess Aphrodite in particular as defined by sexual feeling; it is she who loves the hunter Adonis, gored to death by a wild boar and mourned in Shakespeare's *Venus and Adonis*. She sets desire for one another in the breasts of male lovers, desire that brings both pleasure and pain. Sophocles was reported to have said at the end of his life that he, an old man in his eighties, was glad finally to be relieved of Aphrodite's torments, the pangs of longing and lust.

In the polytheistic world of ancient Greece, sexual passion was the domain of Aphrodite; she was desire, she caused it, directed it, and governed it as a crucial part of human experience. She ruled as a powerful force, one to be respected and reckoned with, since she took her revenge on those who failed to honor her. With her son Eros, the boy "Desire," she worked everywhere, among the gods, among the animals, and among all humans, implanting lust and in some the urge toward procreation, ensuring the continuity of existence. The Greeks revered and also feared this aspect of human life embodied in the goddess, the power of sexual desire. In some cities, including Corinth, there may have been prostitutes in the temples of Aphrodite, so that travelers could worship the goddess by engaging in sexual intercourse with her priestesses. Such ideas may seem foreign to us, but in fact they are as much a part of our heritage, of the legacy of Western civilization, as the dialogues of Plato, where sexual desire also plays its part, a part sometimes suppressed in scholarly and popular accounts of the history of philosophy. The Greeks acknowledged with a certain awe the power of eros, divinized in the name of Aphrodite, and took account of its sacred effects on everyday life.

Just as the Greeks worshiped a goddess of sexual desire, of the force that fuels sexual intercourse as well as reproduction, so many of them seem to have regarded with interest rather than condemnation sexual practices that are frequently denounced today as essentially "unnatural," contrary to nature and to eternal, natural family values. The idealization of Greek civilization as the fount of Western culture often requires the omission of such crucial features of Greek social life as the public, comic allusion to sexual acts, or the expression of same-sex desire.

Americans still have a list of words that cannot be pronounced on the radio, parts of the human body that cannot be shown on television or in most films, and a call from Christian fundamentalists to conceal human sexuality, not to engage in sex education in schools, and not to distribute condoms in prisons, because sex itself is associated with sin. While lacking the abstract concept of "sexuality," the classical Greeks had words for the sexual organs, for acts of intercourse, obscene names for some sexual positions, and a plural noun, "the things of Aphrodite," *ta aphrodisia,* used to refer to the domain of the goddess. Their ideas about a boundary between the private and the public were more compelling than a sense of crime or impiety in relation to sexual acts. They had little notion of "sin," of essential evil in transgression against a law of God; there was no single god watching and judging their behavior in this domain of experience. They seem to have found public references to sex acts of various sorts amusing, perhaps in the way some of us apparently find flatulence comic when performed in public. They had ideas of appropriateness, of the necessity of respecting sacred space, for example, and of the division between public and private, yet most Greeks apparently thought that in the public performances of comedy it was funny to speak of what was sexual, scatological, and generally obscene; to hear such language in the city's open-air theater, at religious and political festivals, was pleasurable and won the comic playwrights prizes.

I have to perform the laborious and unamusing task of explaining some sexual humor, in order to show what I mean here. Aristophanes, the great comic poet, makes the following jokes, among many others, in his comedies, performed for the assembled city of Athens in honor of the god Dionysus. The Greek word *thuein* literally means "sacrifice," "make an offering to the gods," by cooking meat or pouring drink to the gods, or sacrificing, ritually killing an animal victim. In comedy, the meaning is often extended to mean "have sexual intercourse," in an interesting comment on the power relations between sexual partners. In Aristophanes's comedy the *Acharnians,* one of the characters compliments a girl by saying she'll make a fine piggy sacrifice to Aphrodite (792); in the jokes of comedy, the female sexual organs were often likened to piglets. In Aristophanes's *Birds,* grain was sacrificed to the "phal-eris" bird (565), in a reference to the *phallos,* the free-standing and erect male organ that is depicted on many works of art as well as in the padded costume of comic actors. In Aristophanes's *Lysistrata* (191) the female character Kalonike wants to cut up and swear an oath by a "white horse"; this too is a reference to the *phallos,* an appropriate sacrificial victim for the lustful women of this play. The mention of the horse in this context may, as elsewhere, suggest the sexual position of a woman on top; women in such sexual acts are seen as riders, and references to Amazons, the mythic horsewomen of antiquity, sometimes have a comic sexual meaning. In the *Lysistrata,* the name of the character Rhodippe, which means "rose-horse," probably combines a reference to the female and the male genitals. A husband in the *Lysistrata,* tormented with desire for his wife, is driven wilder by her bringing "rose" perfume to their improvised bed; she later runs away and leaves him with an erection. All these jokes, references to religious practices, to sexual acts of various sorts and to organs, to delight in the body and in its variety of behaviors, took place on stage in the center of the city, and the city itself awarded a prize to the best comic playwright of the season. References to excrement, to farting, to erections, to genitalia, to sexual intercourse, all routinely took place in the comic theater.

Scholars have written about the ways in which Greek tragedy brought the city and its citizens together, almost literally conjuring the *polis* into being by drawing its people into an audience that watched the acting-out of stories from the legendary past, stories from Homer's *Iliad,* from the far distant history of the city, tales of kings, warriors, heroes, and gods. Comedy too was part of the political experience of the city, fostered, encouraged, and paid for by the citizens. A committee of Athenians read the comic plays submitted in a given year, after which a wealthy citizen paid for the training of actors and a chorus to perform the winning scripts. Another committee of the city judged which of the plays in a given festival were best, and awarded prizes for tragedies and comedies. Comedies included not only lots of joking about bodies, sex, and excrement; they also touched on the politics of the city, insulting powerful politicians and public figures, accusing them of various crimes against their fellow citizens. In Aristophanes's *Clouds,* for example, the character Strepsiades, mocking the philosopher Socrates and his students, says he wants to share "a certain little thing," that is, his penis, with Socrates's students (197); he alludes to the commonplace that Socrates's students and his circle in general were given to having sex with one another. Such remarks were quite definitely considered fit for public consumption, not hidden away in shame. In fact, citizens were actually paid to attend the theater in the classical period. Although we sometimes think of the Greek theater as Greek tragedy alone, in fact the audiences at comedies were being educated in the ways of their city, their social responsibilities, and the sexual practices of their community just as were the audiences of tragedy. And the city itself sponsored and encouraged their attendance.

Greek vases often bore images of sexual activity that are still censored or censured in contemporary America. When I recently taught a course on ancient cultures, I wanted to show slides of Greek vases to the lecture hall, filled with about two hundred freshmen. Since there had recently been an incident in which a teacher had been accused of sexual harassment because he had shown students images they considered pornographic, I announced that some people might be offended by these images, and that if anyone feared offense, he or she should leave the hall. I waited; no one left. Peer pressure, or interest? You be the judge. On Greek vases we saw scenes with satyrs and sileni, the companions of the god of wine Dionysos, their bodies with human and animal parts and immense erections, pursuing women. There are scenes of their overpowering and rape of nymphs or mortal women, scenes of banquets or symposia in which groups of people, men with women, men with men, perform various sexual acts with each other in twosomes or in more extended chains. Women perform oral sex on men, men penetrate women vaginally and anally; men penetrate each other. There are scenes of a woman with a basket of phalluses or dildos, another watering a crop of phalluses or dildos, perhaps growing in the ground, a woman running with a giant phallus; scholars differ on whether these representations of detached penises are ritual objects or sex toys. Unlike Greek comedy, vases were often made for private consumption, but they are so numerous that they must have been widely available in the ancient city of Athens, and were sent abroad as well, exported to markets in Italy, for example, where Athenian ceramic art was much appreciated.

Many of these erotic scenes appear on those shapes of vases used for drinking wine, and would have been used at symposia or banquets. The Greeks associated such sexual pleasures with wine, the great gift of Dionysos. The chorus of Euripides's *Bacchae* says of the god:

These blessings he gave:
laughter to the flute
and the loosing of cares
when the shining wine is spilled
at the feast of the gods,
and the wine-bowl casts its sleep
on feasters crowned with ivy.
(*Bacchae,* 379–85, trans. Arrowsmith)

We could read many ancient vases as hymns of praise to Dionysos and his gifts to humankind. Theirs is a crucial domain of ancient Greek experience, another important part of social, political, aesthetic, and philosophical experience. Although the images on some of these vases may not reflect actual behavior on such occasions, the vase painters exhibit no reluctance about the representation of many different sorts of sexual acts, homosexual as well as heterosexual.

Greek sexuality is a complicated matter, one of whose features is a variety of attitudes about homosexuality different from our own. The Athenian philosopher Plato, student of Socrates, so revered by both Allan Bloom and William Bennett, seems to have been a lover of boys, although this interesting fact is often elided in discussion of his work and its import for our own day. Plato, for example, in giving us the extended portrait of Socrates that is his work, the dialogues, often alludes to the practice of pederasty, taking it for granted as a path toward the philosophical life. Pederasty was an institution of the ancient city in which an older man, in love with an adolescent, gave him gifts, pursued him, educated him in the ways of the city, in politics, sometimes had sex with him, and in which the younger man may have either enjoyed or tolerated these attentions because of the benefit he derived from the older man's care for him. See, for example, this passage spoken by Socrates, from one of Plato's most beautiful and influential dialogues, the *Phaedrus*:

> "And now that he has come to welcome his lover and to take pleasure in his company and converse, it comes home to him what a depth of kindliness he has found, and he is filled with amazement, for he perceives that all his other friends and kinsmen have nothing to offer in comparison with this friend in whom there dwells a god. So as he continues in this converse and society, and comes close to his lover in the gymnasium and elsewhere, that flowing stream which Zeus, as the lover of Ganymede, called the 'flood of passion,' pours in upon the lover." (*Phaedrus* 255bc)[21]

This is the same Plato after whom the buffalo, the voice of William Bennett, is named in the televised version of the *Book of Virtues*.

Some of the most exciting and important work in the field of classics in recent years has been done in the area of ancient sexuality. Debates rage about whether there is such a category in ancient culture, whether sexuality can usefully be separated from other areas of experience in ancient societies. (See the section entitled "More Reading.") Sexual acts are seen by some as the occasion for mastery of the self, rather than as a separate part of human existence. Some scholars see pederasty, the male-male sexual tutelage of the ancient city, as a phenomenon with a specific relationship to the Greeks' ideas about politics and mastery, rather than as proof of the constancy of homosexuality in all cultures in all historical periods. Plato seems to have believed in the power of eros between male lovers while arguing against the physical expression of such passion for those with philosophical ambitions. In any case, the claims that homosexual relations are always condemned in civilized societies, or that they demonstrate or lead inevitably to the degeneration of the culture in which they are to be found, are definitively disproven by their widespread practice in ancient Athens, by those very citizens who invented democracy, fought against the barbarians, built the Parthenon, and wrote *Oedipus Rex* and the dialogues of Plato. The men of the leisured class of ancient Athens frequented the gymnasia, watched young men exercise naked, admired, courted, and pursued them, made love to them with their parents' knowledge, and initiated them into the political life of the city. Athenian democracy was thought to have been restored or even founded by the lovers Harmodios and Aristogeiton, male lovers who killed the son of the tyrant Peisistratos in the sixth century, and whose statue adorned the city. The Athenians celebrated a Zeus who, seeing Ganymede on the slopes of Mount Ida, transformed himself into an eagle and carried off this beautiful boy to be his cupbearer, eternally youthful, on Mount Olympus. Although some Athenians, like the comic poet Aristophanes, mocked an adult man who was the passive, receiving partner in homoerotic sex, and there were legal limitations placed on the rights of free boys who prostituted themselves and took money for sex, we find comparatively little evidence of widespread societal disapproval of the practice of pederasty. As we have seen in the dialogues of Plato, this was considered by some thinkers to be customary and even ennobling when it led to participation in philosophical life.

Ancient Greece was certainly not a sexual utopia. Slaves were always subject to sexual domination by their masters, women were strictly forbidden any expression of adulterous interest and in comedy, for example, were mocked for being driven by a lust incapable of self-mastery. But if hierarchical forms of power were often expressed through sexual relations, there was a recognition of eros's power in ancient culture that offers an implicit critique of much hypocrisy and normative policing that characterize the sexual relations of power in our own society.

In another of his virtuous stories, William Bennett records a story of male heroism from classical antiquity. Bennett's version elides the possible homoerotic subtext of this tale, taken from Greek history. He precedes the story of "The Brave Three Hundred," in the section called "Courage," with these remarks: "The Spartans' heroic stand against overwhelming odds inspired the Greeks in later resistance and forever made Sparta's name synonymous with courage" (472–73). As the vast Persian army, led by the emperor Xerxes, invaded Greece in 480, a handful of Spartans occupied the northern pass at Thermopylae hoping to stem the tide. They fought, were betrayed by a Greek who showed the Persians a way around the pass, then stood a whole day holding back the invaders until not a single Spartan was left alive. They delayed the Persians long enough so that the rest of the Greeks, waiting anxiously in the south, could assemble their forces, resist, and eventually, after years of battles, send the Persians back again to Persia.

This is indeed a story of great military achievement. The society of Sparta had directed itself assiduously to the training of its male citizens, partly in order to control and dominate a subject serf population, inculcating in its soldiers endurance, loyalty, and militarism. Herodotus records the epitaph of those Spartans who died at Thermopylae:

Stranger, go tell the Spartans that here
we lie, obedient to their commands.
(*Histories* 7.227)

The Vietnam War film *Go Tell the Spartans* alludes to this episode of Spartan military glory.

What interests me most about the American version of the Spartan victory is what is suppressed or left out of some contemporary retellings of the narrative recorded in Herodotus's *Histories*. The Persian emperor Xerxes, while preparing his attack on the pass at Thermopylae, had sent a spy to observe and report back to him concerning the Spartan troops and their preparations for battle. The spy crept up on them and saw the Spartans outside the defense wall, their weapons set aside; some of them were naked, exercising, some combing their hair. He was astonished. Xerxes, when he heard the report, found their behavior laughable, absurd, and couldn't believe that these men were preparing to kill or be killed. His Greek advisor warned him that he should take these men very seriously indeed:

"I already told you about these men as we were setting out against Greece. You laughed at me for seeing that things would turn out just as they have. I keep trying to tell you the truth, Your Majesty, but it's a struggle. Listen to me now. Those men came here to fight with us for this pass, and that's what they are getting ready to do. It's their way. They groom their hair whenever they are about to risk their lives." (*Histories* 7. 209)

To us this may seem a strange practice, combing and grooming the hair before battle. But it is consistent with Spartan military traditions. One impulse, that of appearing beautiful in death, may have determined the soldiers' actions in this scene. But there is also the related possibility that these soldiers were lovers. The late writer Athenaeus says that before battle the Spartans sacrificed to Eros, "since safety lies in the love of those ranged alongside each other" (13.561e). One of the forces compelling military heroism in Sparta and other cities, including Thebes, was male homosexual eros. In Xenophon's *Symposium,* the philosopher Socrates cites Pausanias, lover of the poet Agathon: "the most valiant army would be one recruited of lovers and their favorites. For these would be most likely to be prevented by shame from deserting one another" (8.35). He adds that both the Thebans and the Eleans followed this policy, sharing common beds and assigning their lovers places alongside them in the battle line. In his life of the Theban general Pelopidas, Plutarch reports:

> Gorgias, according to some, first formed the Sacred Band of three hundred chosen men, to whom, as being a guard for the citadel, the State allowed provision, and

all things necessary for exercise: and hence they were called the city band, as citadels of old were usually called cities. Others say that it was composed of young men attached to each other by personal affection, and a pleasant saying of Pammens is current, that Homer's Nestor was not well skilled in ordering an army, when he advised the Greeks to rank tribe and tribe, and family and family together . . . but that he should have joined lovers and their beloved. For men of the same tribe or family little value one another when dangers press; but a band cemented by friendship grounded upon love is never to be broken, and invincible; since the lovers, ashamed to be base in sight of their beloved, and the beloved before their lovers, willingly rush into danger for the relief of one another. Nor can that be wondered at since they have more regard for their absent lovers than for others present; as in the instance of the man who, when his enemy was going to kill him, earnestly requested him to run him through the breast, that his lover might not blush to see him wounded in the back.[22]

Philip of Macedon, father of Alexander the Great, defeated this formerly unbeaten "sacred band" of Theban warriors, and wept on the battlefield when he found the three hundred men, lovers lying together in death.

Thus the presence of "gays" in the U.S. military, so fiercely opposed by some, finds an analogue in these very ancient traditions, supported not only by Greek military practice, but also by philosophical argument, visible in the very examples of courage most cited by those interested in ancient military history. Such historical detail is suppressed or ignored by those who see in the Greeks only sameness, only their own cultural presuppositions confirmed and validated by a sanitized and bowdlerized account of this ancient society, and by those who reject the Greek practices of homoeroticism, obscenity, and the worship of gods and goddesses delighting in polymorphous eroticism.

5

Democracy

The contemporary right wing often assimilates ancient democracy to our own system of government, and part of the claim that we must persist in our commitment to the exclusive study of *Western* civilization and its writings rests on the claim of continuity and identity between the present and that ancient Greek past. It is important to scrutinize this claim, to look carefully at the very specific form ancient Greek democracy took, so that we might analyze not only the continuities we share with it, but also some of the differences. These differences underscore the unfamiliar beginnings of the institution of democracy, a political system that has often been dehistoricized, either damned or taken for granted and celebrated uncritically in the present.

Many of the institutions of ancient Athenian democracy startle those accustomed to the federal, republican form of government of the United States, which often seems far from a "democracy," rule by the people. The American republic governs through representation, not only because of its vast size, but also because the

founders believed that direct people's rule was dangerous, that only a representative body should make decisions for the people, after election, long deliberation,
and some degree of professionalization. In practice this
has often resulted in politics determined by wealth, a
plutocracy, since only those who can afford to run campaigns requiring vast sums of money, or who can offer
benefits to others who can afford such campaigns, run
for even minor offices in the current political scene.

Winston Churchill said that democracy was merely
the best of many bad systems of governance. But what is
meant by the term democracy? What did it mean in ancient Greece? Ancient Athens in the classical period, especially the fifth century B.C.E., was what political theorists sometimes call a *radical* democracy, from the Latin
root *radix,* meaning "root." The meaning of the word
demokratia, "democracy," derives from the words *demos,*
"people," and *kratia,* "rule"; democracy means "rule by
the people," direct rule. In its radical or "extreme" or
original form, the people ruled. That means among
other things that in ancient Athens all citizens could
vote, in person, in the assembly to which all were invited, on all decisions made by the city. There were features of this democracy that now seem anything but
democratic. Citizenship was strictly controlled, limited
to those men whose fathers, or even fathers *and* mothers, were children of citizens; there was little welcoming
of foreigners, even other Greeks from nearby cities, into

the Athenian citizen body. The citizens of Athens protected the boundaries of the *polis,* the city-state, and membership in the citizen body. They retained for themselves the benefits of belonging to this powerful and relatively wealthy state. Women, slaves, and foreigners, even Greek speakers from other city-states, were prohibited from enjoyment of the privileges and advantages of citizenship.

By the mid-fifth century B.C.E., the Athenians were governing themselves by means of the "radical democracy," as opposed to more moderate forms that preceded it. The tyrants of the sixth century had been deposed. The first tyrant, Peisistratos, mentioned earlier in relation to his sexual practices with the daughter of Megacles, had won power twice, first by cutting himself all over his body and claiming that enemies had attacked him and he needed a bodyguard. With this bodyguard he seized control of the city. He was eventually chased out, but returned to power when he went to a mountain village, dressed up a very tall woman in armor, put her in a chariot, brought her into Athens, and said she was the goddess Athena and wanted him to rule. The people allowed him to take power, perhaps because he represented a counter to traditional aristocratic power and presented them with a pageant, a spectacle, a contract that pleased them, acknowledging the necessity of their approval as he seized power. Eventually he died, his sons were assassinated or defeated, various reforms were instituted, and the full or radical, or "extreme" democracy was established. It remained a difficult balancing act among the anonymous citizens, in theory each equal to the other, the wealthy and powerful, and those gifted speakers, aristocratic and common, who persuaded the people as a whole to act or to refrain from action. The need for new classes of leaders in the democratic city to develop skills in public speaking led to the teaching of rhetoric by such figures as the sophists, traveling lecturers who instructed students on persuasive modes of speech. Rhetoric was seen as a powerful instrument in the hands of men representing new groups in the city, and was sometimes condemned as a dangerously promiscuous skill that could lead the masses in the democratic city astray.

Decisions of this state were made at meetings held in the open air, attended by as many as six thousand people, the number required for certain issues to be decided. In some years there would be forty meetings a year, and at times the meetings lasted for more than a day. The agenda of the meeting would be set by the Boule, a smaller council; that agenda was read at the beginning of the meeting. Any citizen—any free Athenian male enrolled among the citizen body—could speak. Those who spoke often were called the speakers, *rhetores,* but they held no office and were not paid. The police of Athens, slave archers from the distant land of Scythia, used a rope dipped in red coloring to drive those engaged in business in the Agora, the city's marketplace, up onto the Pnyx, an adjacent hill, for meetings of the Assembly. The citizens voted to expand their empire, and to spare or annihilate their enemies, always as a mass influenced by the speeches of their own kind.

The citizens themselves, selected by lot, performed other offices necessary to the functioning of the city, carrying out the decisions of the assembled citizens. This feature of the democracy may seem extraordinary to us; there were no professional mayors, no professional judges, no professional tax collectors. The controlling image for the day-to-day governance of the city was the *kuamos,* the "bean," because the selection of white beans by lot determined those chosen to perform a certain office. There are jokes about this in the comedies of Aristophanes, because a girl's swelling nipples at puberty were referred to as "beans"; to "beanize" was to be ripe for marriage (Ar. Fr. 582). The magistrates of the city were chosen by beans, that is, by lottery. No magistrate could hold the same office twice. There were magistrates to regulate the city's markets, to receive tribute from other cities, there were treasurers of the goddess Athena and other gods, magistrates in charge of paying jurors, fine collectors, magistrates who collected the revenue of the state and who sold property and mining rights, others who administered the prison and death sentences. There were something like five hundred magistracies, held for just one year, so that many citizens had experience of governing and administering the city and its business. There were *arkhontes,* "rulers," chosen by lot after election from the three highest orders of the city, orders based on wealth. An *arkhon* managed the City Dionysia, the city's festival held in honor of Dionysos, where the tragedies and comedies were performed. Another ruler, the "king-*arkhon,*" supervised other religious festivals of Dionysos, and legal cases involving religious offenses. The Polemarch, once the leader of the citizen army in war but later replaced by a board of ten generals, organized the funeral for any soldiers killed in war, and also supervised legal cases involving resident aliens. The magistrates brought cases to juries.

After being chosen by lot, the magistrates were inspected, in a sort of examination of character, to see if they were fit to serve the city. They also underwent an examination at the end of their one-year term. Magistrates who had charge of public money were required to give their accounts to a board of auditors, and would be prosecuted for corruption if the auditors did not release them.

Those who volunteered for jury service made up a body of some six thousand potential jurors, chosen annually. Then the juries were selected by lot from that number to hear individual cases. There were no appointed or elected judges, no professional prosecutors. Citizens brought accusations against others, and argued their cases before the jury; the defendants argued back, and a whole case took just one day. At the end of argument the jurors put pebbles into one of two jars; a simple majority decided the case. If the defendant was convicted, the jurors set the penalty. Jurors were paid to serve in the law courts, and a juror's pay may have provided something like basic economic security for the elderly. Members of the Council were paid too, as were *arkhons* and eventually, all magistrates chosen by lot. A large percentage of the citizen population served the state at any given time, perhaps one sixth. The lowest class of citizens was excluded from some service, and as it was difficult for the rest of the poor to participate fully in all these democratic activities, the city paid them.

The wealthiest citizens gave money to finance certain activities of the city in what were called "liturgies," public services. Among them was the trierarchy, in which a wealthy man "commanded" one of the Athenians' *triremes,* their warships. He was in charge of the maintenance of the *trireme,* required to find and train its crew, at considerable expense. Other liturgies involved sending embassies to religious festivals, to the pan-Hellenic festivals, including the games at Olympia, paying for and training runners for torch races held in honor of the city's own religious festivals, holding a banquet for the festivals of Athena or Dionysos, and choosing, training, paying, and dressing the members of a tragic or comic chorus, and training dancers. Although such payments were a form of indirect taxation, they allowed individuals to choose the intensity of their commitment to these various responsibilities, and some of the wealthy seem to have taken pride in their execution, as in the victories of their choruses in tragic or comic competitions.

Many of the most successful speakers in the Assembly were wealthy and were descendants of noble families which claimed the gods as their ancestors. The Athenians worried that such men might have tyrannical ambitions, and might seek to restore the tyranny of the past. In the sixth century B.C.E., as noted earlier, the powerful Peisistratos had taken over the city and ruled alone, as a monarch. Later his sons had inherited his rule, and were ousted with some difficulty. Perhaps in order to fend off such moves, and to protect the democracy which had grown up after the tyrants had been deposed, the Athenians continued to employ what they called "ostracism," after the *ostrakon,* the oyster shell used as a ballot in a peculiar form of antielection. Each year the Assembly was asked if it wished to hold an ostracism, and if it did, each citizen who wished to do so wrote on a shard of pottery, which had replaced the oyster shell, the name of the person he wanted banished from the city. If there were at least six thousand votes, the person whose name appeared on the greatest number of *ostraka* was exiled. He had to leave the city within ten days, and to stay away for ten years.

This procedure may have been introduced at the end of the sixth century, just after the fall of the tyranny. One of the tyrant's sons was assassinated by two aristocratic youths, Harmodius and Aristogeiton, as mentioned earlier, and the other was deposed and finally joined the Persians, acting as an advisor and witness at the battle of Marathon, where the Athenians led the Greeks to victory over the Persian imperial army. The mechanism of ostracism defended the city against a return of the tyranny, and in this way served democracy. Not only did almost all the officers of the Athenian state work for their city only after having been chosen by lot; the city also worked out this other method of guaranteeing that no one could become too powerful and direct the democracy against its collective will.

There are of course ways in which our governance is more "democratic," if we can use that term abstractly, than that of the ancient Athenians. Women, or at least some women who reside in the United States, can vote; the Athenians did not really consider their women to be citizens, but rather to be the daughters, wives, and mothers of male citizens, and they had no political responsibilities except that of reproducing the corps of male citizens. Foreign women and slaves were usually excluded from mothering citizens, and shared the Athenian women's lack of voting rights. In some ways our system has fulfilled the promise of democracy, the extension of its logic of equality, further than did the ancient city state. Yet, as we have seen, in other ways the ancient democracy was more radical, more confident in citizen-rule than is our own system of governance. In its policies of choosing governors by lot, in its support for the poor and the old, and in payment of a living wage for jurors and for those who served in the city's fleet, the city relied on ordinary citizens, and it further entrusted to the assembled citizen body all political decisions.

Fear of democracy accompanied the birth of the democratic Greek city-state and has left its legacy in the historical record. Although democracy seems in ancient Greece to have meant rule by the people, the citizen body—as opposed to monarchy, tyranny, theocracy, oligarchy, or aristocracy—elite thinkers even in antiquity often understood it to mean rule by the mob, the poor of the city. The great historian Thucydides organized his history of the Peloponnesian War, the war between Athens and Sparta and their allies, around a portrait of the democracy that has influenced political theory since his day, showing a city brought to ruin through charismatic leaders like Alcibiades, a city weak and susceptible to flattery and charm on the part of its noble leaders (2.37). Plato offered a famous and enduring critique of democracy in his *Republic* and elsewhere; this is his description, staged as part of a conversation between

Socrates and Adeimantus, of the character of the "democratic man":

> "And does he not, said I [Socrates], also live out his life in this fashion, day by day indulging the appetite of the day, now winebibbing and abandoning himself to the lascivious pleasing of the flute and again drinking only water and dieting, and at one time exercising his body, and sometimes idling and neglecting all things, and at another time seeming to occupy himself with philosophy? And frequently he goes in for politics and bounces up and says and does whatever enters his head. And if military men excite his emulation, thither he rushes, and if moneyed men, to that he turns, and there is no order or compulsion in his existence, but he calls this life of his the life of pleasure and freedom and happiness and cleaves to it to the end."
> "That is a perfect description," he said, "of a devotee of equality."
> (Plato, *Republic* 561c–e)

The Athenian democracy, which had executed Plato's beloved Socrates, perhaps in part for his association with a group of men implicated in a violent seizure of oligarchic power, met with Plato's disapproval. He condemned rhetoric and rhetorical training as a poor substitute for true philosophical inquiry. Aristotle too expressed fear of demagogues, unscrupulous and manipulative speakers in the assembly who influenced the poorer citizens in a democracy. The danger was that the better classes could no longer dominate in such a situation, and that the mob would be swayed by an appeal to their basest motives. We inherit this perspective on ancient democracy—fear of the poor, of the mob, of demagogues—and books such as Donald Kagan's and Allan Bloom's stress the need for strong leaders, or philosophers, to guide the state and avoid the pitfalls of democratic rule.

A certain strain in ancient philosophy and in its critiques of democracy serves contemporary mythology about the good life, the proper organization of society and politics, and the relationship between the nation and its artists. Plato's banishment of artists and poets from the ideal state is part of this scheme. In Plato's view, neither rhetoricians, nor artists and poets can represent truth. Only philosophers, those trained in the difficult arts of argument and dialectic, can do so. Although he himself was a poet at some stage of his life, Plato seems to have banished artists and poets from his republic because in his view they can represent, at a great remove, only imitations of imitations of the real, the true, and the good, ideas or forms that reside in a metaphysical realm distant from human existence, perhaps in or beyond the realm of the gods. Plato's paradoxical antiart views, expressed by some of the characters in his artful dialogues, accompany his antidemocratic views.

What can the complicated, contested example of ancient democracy reveal about the vexed contemporary problem of the social responsibility of the artist, and the role of the state in support of the arts? Plutarch's account of the classical leader Pericles's great building program for the city of Athens names no artist, stressing instead the distribution of the city's wealth to all through Pericles's efforts:

it was necessary, now that the city was sufficiently supplied with the necessities for war, to devote the surplus of the treasury to the construction of these monuments, from which, in the future would come everlasting fame, and which while in construction, would supply a ready source of welfare by requiring every sort of workmanship. . . . this so that the population at home would have a claim to derive benefit from and have a share in the public funds. For this undertaking the materials used were stone, bronze, ivory, ebony and cypress-wood, and those who labored on them were builders, modellers, bronzeworkers, stone-cutters, dyers, workers in gold and ivory, painters, embroiderers, and engravers. . . . Thus each art, just as each general has his own army under him, had its own private throng of laborers organized like an army, acting as an instrument and body of public service; so, to sum the whole thing up, briefly, the opportunities for service reached every age and type, and they distributed the wealth accordingly. (Plutarch, *Life of Pericles* 12–13)

This state, the radical democracy, committed itelf to the distribution of wealth among its citizens, among them artists and artisans. The "artist" employed by the ancient democracy was a laborer, who often mattered far less than what surrounded the object or monument he made: its donor, its effects, its powers, and its political meaning, established by the democratic Assembly, were often far more important than its maker.

We witness in Greek lyric poetry and in the first signed works of art in Greek antiquity the origins of an ever more evolved individualism. But it would be a mistake to see the naming of individual artists in the ancient world as equivalent to our own art practices, with their celebration of individual genius and of the commodified art object. In the world of classical antiquity, objects themselves had a residual authority, divine or magical, owing something to the legendary Daedalus, that often superseded the recognition of their makers. Ancient works of art and the great architectural building projects of the classical age served as a celebration of the city's or an individual's wealth, as adornment of the city, as recognition of the importance of the gods to the city's well-being, as occasions for the distribution of wealth to citizens, or as gifts of their donors, rather than as an expression of the creative genius of their individual makers.

Perhaps we need to think more about the experience of radical democracy and its effects on the built environment of Athens, for example, rather than accepting the facile conservatism of those who want to appropriate ancient history to justify a political program, citing it like the quotation of ancient pediments on state buildings and on bank facades. If we are to use history to think about the present and the future, study of the democracy of the ancient Greeks raises questions about the place of art in society, about professional artists, their works of art, state support of the arts, and the role of the state as censor. For the Greeks, art was always a matter of politics, always political.

The very unfamiliarity and strangeness of the democracy of the Athenians in the fifth century B.C.E. might still serve as an important source for critique of our own political life. We should be wary of calls to "live like Greeks, think like Greeks." We should be wary of claims that we are simply living out the glorious legacy of ancient democracy, an institution that in fact perpetuated slavery, imperialism, and the torture of slaves. And observing the example of the ancient Athenians, we should be wary of calls to protect our republic from seductive rhetoric and radical democracy through militarism and strong leadership. What is most crucial for me is the recognition of the contradictory, sometimes ambiguous nature of ancient democracy, and the need to resist comforting, simple, and reductive forms of denunciation, identification with, or idealization of the ancient Greek past.

6

Gods

The world of the ancient Greeks was full of gods. This is an unfamiliar notion in a monotheistic world, one dominated by the idea of "God the Father." Americans are accustomed to seeing the account of the evolution of religion in the West as progress from paganism and polytheism to monotheism, its one god a patriarch triumphing over superstition. There follows an often sloppy reliance on the so-called Judeo-Christian tradition, a phrase that obscures great differences, conflict, and the sometimes genocidal domination for many centuries of a Christian majority over a Jewish minority. The appeal in contemporary politics to a common god ignores the many citizens of modern states who do not believe in such a god, and also threatens to overwhelm the separation between so-called church and state that guided the Enlightenment founders of the American republic. And in their appeals to the classical tradition, conservative thinkers often disregard the polytheistic nature of ancient Greek and Roman societies, as much a part of the Western tradition as the invention of philosophy or indeed, as slavery.

Many of the ancient Greeks, those not philosophically or atheistically inclined, believed that the world was replete with divinities of various sorts, that the earth itself, herself, was a goddess, that there was a god present when people exchanged money, that wine was full of a god, its power the presence of the god in the liquid. Perhaps we might think again about whether the notion of a punishing and rewarding father, always watching, marks a progression in human thinking. The Greeks had a reverence for the wild earth, for wildness, for wilderness, for example, that counters later centuries' instrumentalizing conception of the earth as an object to be plundered.

One of the most difficult things to convey in teaching ancient culture is that there was in fact no such thing as ancient Greek mythology, or even religion in our sense. Rather, for many of the ancient Greeks, the gods were everywhere, part of everyday life, every feature of material life, part of what we now divide up into politics, law, literature, and science, as well as religion. The gods were active and present for most people in all these domains of existence; the goddess Athena was the guardian of the city of Athens, the city's architects and artists and artisan workers celebrated and represented her, and poets wrote hymns to her; she protected the Athenians and their city in time of war. And she was a goddess worshiped elsewhere, in other cities as well.

We might see Greek "religion" as a representation of a field of forces. Aphrodite, for example, names the energy of sexuality, not necessarily benevolent, indifferent to human plans, sometimes giving ecstasy, sometimes taking over and racking her victims' bodies. We see her power at work in the poems of Sappho, when the poet describes herself as an oak tossed by winds:

> *Love shook my senses,*
> *like wind crashing on mountain oaks.*[23]

In Athens, Aphrodite, like the rest of the gods, was ubiquitous, present even in the center of the city. The *agora,* like the Roman forum a space for the conduct of business, was set apart from the residences of the Athenians and was separate too from the Acropolis, the hill dominating the city and dedicated to the worship of Athena, goddess of the city itself. In the *agora* were moneylenders, public buildings including a dining hall for the city's officials and long open porches providing shade for political debate and philosophical conversation. Yet even here, in the marketplace and political center of the city, the gods had their place; there were temples and shrines to the god Hephaistos, to the mother of the gods (whose shrine was also a repository of state archives), a later temple dedicated to Apollo, and a porch or portico built in honor of Zeus as the savior of the Athenians from the Persians. Even the *agora* itself, the square, was marked by a boundary stone that designated this space as sacred, and prohibited certain convicts from entering it.

The great tragedian Sophocles, who wrote *Oedipus Rex* and *Antigone,* was renowned for his reverence of the power of the gods. When the Athenians brought the sacred snake of Asklepios, one of the gods of healing, to Athens, it was housed at the home of Sophocles until a proper place at the temple could be arranged for it.

One of the seven wonders of the ancient world was dedicated to goddess worship, the great temple of Artemis at Ephesos, in what is now Turkey. Of all the wonders—the pyramid in Egypt, the hanging gardens of Babylon, the great statue of Zeus at Olympia, the Mausoleum at Halicarnassus, the colossus of Rhodes, the *pharos* or lighthouse at Alexandria—this is the only one that is neither the tomb of a great man, nor a civic monument, nor even the representation of a god. Rather it is a reminder of a once crucial practice of the ancient world, the celebration and worship of female powers. In addition to the patriarchal authority William Bennett finds in the Greeks, there were goddesses of virginity, of wild animals, of the reproductive power of women, cults celebrating the analogy between women's bodies and the fertile earth, celebrating women's labor as weavers, and women's sexual power. There were many aspects of female experience embodied in gods and goddesses, considered powerful energies to be reckoned with and honored.

The German philosopher and classicist Nietzsche wrote something about ancient architecture that reminds me of the link between these powers the Greeks acknowledged, and human beings' building:

> In general we no longer understand architecture. . . .
> [An] atmosphere of inexhaustible meaningfulness hung
> about [an ancient] building like a magic veil. Beauty
> entered the system only secondarily, without impairing
> the basic feeling of uncanny sublimity, of sanctification
> by magic or the gods' nearness. At most the beauty tempered the *dread*—but this dread was the prerequisite
> everywhere. (*Human, All Too Human*)

This mood of dread and sublimity would, I think, have been particularly appropriate to a temple of Artemis.

What is the domain of Artemis's power, what are the "myths," the stories the ancient Greeks told about her and the "religious" practices associated with her worship? And what was the Ephesos temple, one of the greatest sites of ancient cult, of which very little remains, but which is still remembered as one of the seven wonders of the world?

Artemis is the goddess of *wildness*, something that the modern world is in danger of forgetting, of wishing to eradicate, or of nostalgically visiting as it threatens to disappear forever. The power named Artemis by the

Greeks contains an implicit threat—that she will exact a pitiless vengeance from those who transgress. In the Greeks' view, the gods were not sentimental about and not often interested in human beings, unless those human beings violated some sacred space, or were themselves extraordinary, or gave lavish gifts to their gods. Even then, the deities of the Greeks were unreliable. I was reminded of the power of Artemis, of wildness, when I read the reports of climbers stranded on Mount Everest by a blizzard, killed by an unexpected storm. For the Greeks, Artemis watched over nonhuman nature, all that which is unknowable or uncanny; she needed to be respected and placated. The Greeks did not believe that the natural world was organized around or for the benefit of a universal human subject, or that a single patriarchal god had entered into a compact with human beings to privilege them among all other living beings. The natural world existed as a domain unto itself, and it could be hostile and randomly, inadvertently, arbitrarily violent and destructive. Nature, in the name of Artemis, had to be recognized, feared, honored, and revered.

Artemis ruled as a figure for the wild, the untamed, the dangerous and mysterious dimension of the natural world. The Greeks did not sentimentalize nature, didn't really like wandering in the woods, or on the trackless sea, didn't paint "nature" in art, would not have climbed Mount Everest if invited to do so. They liked humanized landscapes, and situated temples in particular landscapes in order to punctuate wild lands, carefully organizing that territory within a human interpretation of space. Raw, unmediated nature and space were seen as threatening to human community, as the domain where the great Artemis reigned, where human beings entered at their peril. Stories about her often reminded them to respect her power.

The figure of Artemis is related to aspects of very ancient goddess worship—to the great mother of the earliest Mediterranean peoples, guardian of the untamed wild lands and mother of wild beasts. Some scholars believe that the earliest Western art, Paleolithic paintings in caves, may have been drawn to adorn the inner spaces of her body, to impregnate her, and encourage her to bear animals for the hunt, that dangerous enterprise in which human beings had to engage in order to acquire meat for survival. There are some later but still ancient representations of this figure, with breasts from which protruded eagles' beaks, and examples from the Near East of powerful, wild, sometimes sexual goddesses. There are still later Cretan figures of the "mistress of the animals," images of a tree and a goddess with subject animals on each side. The Minoans of Crete, site of Daedalus's labyrinth, made figurines of a female with snakes for bracelets, belts, and necklaces, with attendant animals on her head.

The Greek goddess Artemis probably evolved from these goddesses; it's possible that Olympian Greek religion, the worship of the classical age, represents a synthesis of early goddess worship with the religion of invading Greek speakers who entered the Mediterranean basin in prehistory. Some scholars believe that the earliest religion of the Mediterranean region focused on cults of goddesses, goddesses of fertility, of animals, and of the earth, and that these were subordinated in those areas where the earliest Greek speakers arrived. They may have brought about the domination in cult of goddesses by sky gods, the relative reduction of the power of female divinities in comparison to that of patriarchal gods like Ouranos, "Sky," and Zeus, the patriarch of the Greek Olympian gods. The replacement of an earlier divinity at the Delphic oracle by the Olympian Apollo may be traced to this historic change. Yet the Greeks continued to honor and worship female deities, goddesses signifying the power of fields to grow food, of female bodies to reproduce, or of such a goddess as Artemis to watch over wild things, even though in the classical age mortal women were kept strictly in their places by citizen husbands and fathers.

Artemis represents an archaic and very ancient dimension of the world—wildness, free and elemental. Abiding in the uncivilized places, watching, protecting wild animals and wild space from intrusion or violation, she stands for the virginal, asexual power of women, a divinity devoted to saving her creatures and her lands from rape by men. She is represented as remote and incorruptible. But if she protects the wild animals, she is also their huntress. These are lines from an early poem sung in honor of the goddess, the *Homeric Hymn to Artemis*:

> *. . . through shady mountains and windy peaks*
> *she delights in the chase as she stretches her golden bow*
> *to shoot the bitter arrows. The crests of tall mountains*
> *tremble, and the thick-shaded forest resounds*
> *dreadfully with the cries of beasts, while the earth*
> *and the fishy deep shudder. Hers is a mighty heart,*
> *and she roams all over destroying the brood of wild beasts.*

If her domain is wilderness, she exercises her right both to give life and to take it.

The goddess of wild animals, the hunt, is also the goddess of adolescent, presexual human animals. Puberty and sexual initiation were seen as a kind of taming by the Greeks, a domestication of young human beings' nature, their wildness. Before this taming, human children were likened to wild animals, not gendered, running free; Artemis watched over them. And she could also destroy them. The Greeks told the story of Niobe, a human woman who boasted that she had borne more children, seven boys and seven girls, than Leto, the goddess mother of Artemis and her brother Apollo. In retribution, all fourteen of Niobe's children were killed with Leto's children's arrows, and Niobe herself was turned to stone, pointed to in the landscape of Asia Minor in the form of a weeping mountain.

One of the practices associated with the myths and cult of Artemis was human sacrifice; in the classical age it was probably understood as having been performed only in the past, but was recalled as a ritual which evoked Artemis's worshipers' respect and awe. I mention all this not to suggest that we return to the worship of Artemis, nor to human sacrifice, but rather that we acknowledge the disturbing unfamiliarity of the Greeks' ways of dealing with the complicated, difficult nature of human existence on this earth. They registered fear and dread and awe and the sorrow of life and death in sometimes sprawling and contradictory narratives, in myths and tragedies, instead of reducing such matters to the shallow oversimplification we find in many domains of contemporary life, fantasies of consumer satisfaction or the deferral of happiness until the afterlife.

The stories—or myths—told about Artemis take up the themes of wildness, of the uncanny, of the difficulties of adolescence, virginity, and sacrifice. Artemis, although probably a pre-Greek figure—pre-Hellenic— was in the classical period identified as the daughter of Zeus by Leto, and as the twin sister of the god Apollo. She was said to have killed the hunter Orion for insulting her, that same Orion who survives in the night sky as a constellation. Actaeon, the hunter of the house of Thebes, caught sight of Artemis once while hunting, and because of this inadvertent sacrilege was turned into a stag by the goddess and then torn apart by his own dogs. Artemis protected her own virginity and that of her attendants; her virginity is not of the sort to be recognized as a "virtue" by a thinker such as William Bennett. Artemis was capable of violence and rage when human beings violated her domain. Before the Trojan War, that great combat between Greeks and Trojans over the possession of Helen, the Greek fleet at Aulis, eager to sail to Troy and capture Helen, ran afoul of Artemis. Agamemnon, commander of the Greek forces, waiting for the others to arrive at Aulis in northern Greece, killed a deer during a hunt. According to various versions of the myth, he claimed superiority over Artemis as a hunter, or the deer was sacred, or the goddess's sanctuary was violated. Another account says that he had promised to Artemis the first fruits, a sort of tithe, when his daughter Iphigeneia was born. Artemis demanded the sacrifice of his daughter, and held back the winds from Aulis so the Greeks' fleet could not sail to Troy. Agamemnon eventually complied with the goddess's demands; he lured Iphigeneia to Aulis, promising marriage with Achilles, and cut her throat at the altar of Artemis. The winds returned and the fleet sailed to Troy. Agamemnon won his wife Klytemnestra's undying hatred for this sacrifice to Artemis. In another variation on this story, a less ruthless Artemis substituted a deer for Iphigeneia, the daughter, and took Iphigeneia to Asia Minor, to Tauris, to serve as a priestess of Artemis's cult.

♦

The rituals and cult practices of worship of Artemis seem consistent with the Greeks' sense of her ferocity and her desire for vengeance, with her commitment to the destruction of those who opposed her, and her ambiguous protection and pursuit of the young and the wild. At Halae worshipers performed a ritual that recalled human sacrifice—a few drops of blood were drawn from a man's throat with a sword. At Brauron, near Athens, little girls dressed as bear cubs in Artemis's honor and danced before the goddess. The children, prepubescent, were under her protection, like wild animals, nurtured but also subject to the hunt. At Brauron Artemis was also worshiped as sacred to women in childbirth. Here too her role seems to us ambiguous; she protected some but brought death to others. Artemis embodies the violence of natural existence, the dangers of childbirth, the vulnerability of children, and their unsocialized affinity with wild animals.

In the Greek city of Patras worshipers of Artemis set up a table of offerings or an altar of dry wood surrounded by green, less flammable wood. The sacrificers then assembled animals gathered in a hunt conducted in Artemis's honor; they filled the platform with wild game held down by nets and ropes. Then the priestesses of Artemis ignited the platform, and the celebrants danced around it, while the animals burned and the head priestess presided in a chariot drawn by stags, like Artemis's own chariot.

Among Artemis' worshipers were the legendary Amazons. These women formed a society apart, one of female warriors, always located at the boundaries of the known world. They lived an existence separate from men, meeting other tribes to breed and then banishing or killing or sometimes disabling their male children. They were hunters and fighters, rode horses, and used Artemis's weapon, the bow. They were said to have come to Troy to help the Trojans against the Greeks. Achilles killed their queen Penthesilea, but fell in love with her as he pierced her body with his spear; this moment is represented on a famous vase. Amazons were a favorite subject in art. So different from Greek women, they wore highly decorated leggings, carried weapons, and rode to battle on horseback; they appear on many vases and adorn the sculpture of many temples. One of the canonical twelve labors of Herakles involves the Amazons; he was sent on an expedition to acquire their queen Hippolyta's belt. Theseus, the great Athenian hero who traveled with him, was said to have stolen not the belt but the queen herself. Shakespeare's *Midsummer Night's Dream* takes place in the couple's Athenian court. The Amazons, according to Greek legend, came to Athens to get their queen back, camped on the Areopagus, where Saint Paul later preached to the Athenians, and were defeated there. The great god Dionysos, god of wine and all things wet, was also said to have fought and defeated the Amazons. Another legend claimed that the Amazons were the founders of the city of Ephesos in Asia Minor, site of the great temple of Artemis that was to become one of the seven wonders of the ancient world.

In sculptural representations on the temple of Bassae in Arcadia, on the Athenian treasury at Delphi, on the Parthenon, the great temple of Athena and of Athens, the battle between the Greeks and the Amazons represented the conflict between Hellenic civilization and barbarism, just as did its frequent companion in art, the fight between the Lapiths, a tribe of human beings, and the Centaurs, half-horses, half-men, hyperphallic, wild, bestial, and in certain respects barbaric like the Amazons.

The situation of the great temple of Artemis at the site of Ephesos, in Asia Minor, brought it close to those the Greeks deemed barbarians—Persians, Lydians, all the peoples of the ancient Near East who were not Greek speakers, had different gods, different customs, and a history of huge empires ruled by despots who themselves resembled gods or their priests. These are the peoples who fascinated the early historian and ethnographer Herodotus, and whom he describes in some of the books of his history. The worship of Artemis was carried on at this great site far from the centers of Hellenic life in Athens, Olympia, and Delphi, at the margins, at the boundaries with the non-Greeks, those others who both intrigued and repelled the Greeks.

Ephesos was a site of mixture, of the mingling of Greek and barbarian, like much of Asia Minor. The city's worship of Artemis was said to derive from its foundation by the Amazons traveling from their lands in the further north and east. Others said the worship of Artemis there was based on an image, an idol found in a marsh, perhaps in fact a meteorite, a shapeless, wild, uncivilized object, not a work of human art. Artemis there took on aspects of Asiatic goddesses as well as her customary attributes from mainland Greece. Her devotees seem to have incorporated features of the worship of the mother goddess of Phrygia, Kybele, and associated her with the Magna Mater, the great mother goddess. In a very early deposit on the site of the later temple at Ephesos, archaeologists found archaic figures with Lydian, Persian, Phrygian, Hittite, Assyrian, and Egyptian features, indicating connections with all these "barbarian" cultures of Asia and Africa.

There were actually two important temples at the site in Ephesos, the first known as temple D, or the Croesus building, named after Croesus, the Lydian monarch legendary for his wealth—some of the columns were erected at his expense between 560 and 546 B.C.E., and carry his name on the base. Artemis was the goddess of this sanctuary. Herodotus, the first historian, tells this story about the goddess's failure to protect the city, at the time when Croesus was seeking to enlarge his kingdom:

> The first Greek city that Croesus attacked was Ephesos. The Ephesians, when he laid siege to them, ran a rope from their walls to the temple of Artemis, putting the town, by means of this link, under the goddess' protection. (Herodotus, *Histories* 1.26)

But the city fell. The victor Croesus, in his great wealth, sent massive offerings of gold and precious objects to the shrine of Apollo at Delphi, the site of Apollo's oracle. Later, when he was about to be burned by the Persian emperor Xerxes, who had in his turn conquered Lydia, Croesus called on Apollo to rescue him, and Apollo sent a saving rain to put out the fire. The gods sometimes, not always, remembered and protected those who had been generous toward them. Subsequently the Persian emperor Xerxes, after his defeat by the Greeks, sent his children for sanctuary to the temple of Artemis, where they were guarded by his admiral, commander of her own fleet, queen Artemisia, named for the goddess.

This temple of Artemis was said to have been built by Chersiphron of Knossos, on Crete, and his son Metagenes. They set its foundations on charcoal and fleece because of the marshy ground where the mysterious figurine of Artemis, said to have fallen from the heavens, was first found. These architects wrote a book about its construction, now lost, one of the very early prose works in Greek, indicating the importance of architecture, the daedalic art, in ancient Greek culture. They were reported to have told stories of their despair at the difficulties of raising the great slab for the central architrave, the lintel of the temple. In the middle of one night Artemis herself lifted the huge stone into place.

The temple, immense, was said like an Egyptian temple to resemble a forest, a grove of trees, and was thus a building fusing a wild forested landscape with the orderliness of human construction. The total number of columns in the peristyle, the colonnade, was one-hundred six. The inner room, the cella, may have been open to the sky, and contained a sacred pool, another sign of wilderness or natural forces contained within the fabric of the temple. It had the curled capitals of Ionic columns, some with sculptured lower drums. It is thought that these columns were transported by building wood frames and wheels around them; then the architects rolled them to the temple site. The architrave or lintel must have been very large, since it took Artemis herself to lift it. There was apparently a parapet with monsters or Gorgons on the four corners. A contest was held among artists to commemorate the foundation of the city by the woman warrior Amazons; the four best bronze statues of Amazons were chosen to decorate the temple. This temple, the earlier building on the site, was burned down in 356 B.C.E. by a man named Herostratos on the night of the birth of Alexander the Great. Artemis, goddess of childbirth, could not protect her own temple from destruction. Its burning was interpreted as one of those many signs that mark the birth of a great hero, like the star over Bethlehem in later history.

Artemis's Temple E was built in this earlier temple's place, and became the most important temple in Asia Minor. Rebuilt immediately with a plan like that of the former temple, it was even more splendid, constructed on a higher platform, again using the idea of sculptured columns. It may have been the beauty of these columns, perhaps rendered by Scopas, that made it one of the seven wonders. This second temple's architects were Paeonius of Ephesos and Demetrius "the slave of Artemis." This second temple reportedly took one hundred twenty years to build, and was not completed until 236 B.C.E. When Alexander the Great came through on his great journey of conquest, he asked to be allowed to contribute to the costs of its construction and to receive in turn the inscription of his name on the temple; he was politely refused this honor, a citizen telling him tactfully that one god did not make offerings to another.

This second temple had an identical ground plan to that of the archaic temple, but it was set higher off the ground, reached by fourteen steps rather than two, and adorned by thirty-six sculptured columns. Visitors would again have been struck by the impression of en-

tering a forest of columns, resolving the contrast between inside and outside, nature and culture, wildness
and artifice. Artemis's temple may have seemed to con-
tain an inner forest, one sheltered and constructed, built
by human ingenuity to honor this goddess of wild
spaces. And this building too may have been only par-
tially roofed, with a central area open to the sky.

This temple has also disappeared. But it had a great
facade, a heavy lintel, lacking the frieze many temples
bore; commentators mention the weight of its pediment, the three windows left in the tympanum, in the
triangle of the pediment. It was probably covered with
statues of Amazons. And the goddess Artemis may have
shown herself to worshipers in the course of ritual cele-
brations; there seems to have been a window for her appearance. The facade of this temple appears on coins
with the figure of Artemis *polymaste,* "Artemis of the
many breasts," which became the canonical representation of the Ephesian Artemis or Diana. This figure is
one of the most interesting features of the worship of
Artemis; Artemis is covered with many breasts, or many
eggs, or perhaps, as some scholars now believe, with
many bull's testicles; the goddess bore these signs of fertility and potency, even though she herself remained a
virgin. Beneath the many "breasts" appeared other creatures—deer, sirens, bees, lions, sphinxes, and griffins—
in relief. The statue of the goddess is thus a repository of
these signs of animal nature and of the hybrid creations

of human storytelling or myth. In the altar court outside the temple where sacrifices were performed, worshipers stood waiting for the appearance of the goddess or priestess at the window.

The great historian of architecture Vincent Scully describes the effect the temple might have had on worshipers:

The temple itself faced out to sea, but at an angle which brought into the goddess' focus the great horns [mountains] above Klaros across the bay. . . . Standing within her cella, the mother of all the creatures on the continent looked out through the shadows of her colonnade to the approaching traveler. . . . the wide spreading colonnade must be seen as a forest through which the labyrinthine processions wound. The shafts of the columns would then have acted in the way that the reliefs upon them indicate and express: as the definers of a curving, unilinear movement which coils around them. At the same time the wings of Artemis are echoed by the winged mountained profile that flanks the site. . . . there were so many columns that there must have been a tendency on the part of the participant to wander among them and an invitation for a procession to move in a ceremonial dance . . . but around the abstract white pavilion in which the dance took place rose the embracing arc of the continent's hills. Therefore, while the open altar, the image, the wide platform, and the grove of Artemis are down in the swampy lands, one feels that they are invoking not only the water forces from which they spring but also that presence who sits, as in the caves of Crete or like the rock-cut Hittite goddess on Mount Sipylos, high above and beyond them among the peaks.[24]

This temple marked an extraordinary boundary between human order and the other order that was the gods', a threshold between the sea and the land, between the West and the East, where civilization met barbarism, and humanity encountered the unknowable forces of nature deified in Artemis.

Antipater, a Greek poet of about 140 B.C.E., described his awe at the sight of this great temple:

I have gazed on the walls of impregnable Babylon, along which chariots may race, and on the Zeus by the banks of the Alphaeus. I have seen the Hanging Gardens and the Colossus of Helios, the great man-made mountains of the lofty pyramids, and the gigantic tomb of Mausolos. But when I saw the sacred house of Artemis that towers to the clouds, the others were placed in the shade, for the sun himself has never looked upon its equal outside Olympus.

This great goddess Artemis was just one of the many divinities who inhabited the religious imagination of the ancient Greeks, whose worship demanded an alert and reverent attention to their multiple powers. Worship of these deities saturated the Greeks' ideas about space, about human kinds and gender differences, about life, death, and politics.

◆

The city of Ephesos in Asia Minor, where the temple of Artemis stood, was a great banking center for centuries; wealthy, it teemed with merchants, artisans, actors, singers, fortune-tellers and magicians, priests and priestesses, and remained a prosperous center of prostitution. The New Testament book of *Acts* records St. Paul's visit to the city; when he preached against the idols of the silversmiths, who sold images of the goddess to pilgrims visiting the great temple of Artemis-Diana, the crowd shouted back at him: "Great is Diana of the Ephesians" (*Acts* 19, 24–34).

The striking syncretism of early Christianity could not inculcate absolute patriarchal monotheism without encountering this sort of resistance. Cultic devotion to another virgin was instituted at Ephesos, in a historical process that undermines the claims of revelation and monotheism in contemporary orthodox fundamentalist Christianity. According to legend, Mary, Jesus' mother, came to live there under the care of John after the death of Jesus. One tradition holds that the assumption of Mary to heaven took place from Ephesos, another that a nineteenth-century German mystic, Catherine Emmerich, had visions of the house and tomb of the Virgin Mary at Ephesos, a place she had never visited. Archaeologists who excavated the site she described uncovered a tiny first-century house, which they declared to be Mary the Virgin Mother's. Pilgrims venerate another such house in Italy, at Loreto, where it is said to have been miraculously transported from Ephesos. The divine virgin thus persists: "Great is Diana of the Ephesians."

Rather than observing patriarchal monotheism, the Greeks rejoiced in their polytheism, in a multiplicity of powers and presences that enabled thinking about the mysteries of war and peace, young and old, nature and civilization, friends and enemies, male and female, birth and death. Artemis is just one of the gods of the Greek pantheon. The world full of gods of the Greeks sacralized space and the events of human existence. Dionysos was in the wine, Hermes traveled with the traveler, Demeter watched over the fields, the grain, and the fertile bodies of the city's women.

Greek polytheism was not the strained tolerance of a society that allowed some people to worship a single god, others to worship another. The Greeks were not obliged by their gods to choose among them. Their world, full of gods and goddesses, demanded various sorts of attention—battle, buildings, prayers, sacrifices, offerings, or songs of gratitude and praise. The gods of the Greeks were thought to appreciate such human efforts and occasionally to punish transgressions. Apollo rewarded Croesus, Artemis destroyed Actaeon, Dionysos punished those aristocrats, in myth, who denied his power or refused his gift of wine. But if the gods' notice and recognition of human effort or oblivion were intermittent, the negative side of their vengeance was balanced by gifts humans needed, the gift of intoxication from Dionysos, of nourishment from Demeter, or of the animals of the hunt from Artemis. Ancient religion was not a monolith, but multifaceted, dynamic, and changing over time, a source of disparate beginnings for those who followed.

I have offered this brief account of some features of ancient Greek sex, politics, and religion in order to point toward a more nuanced, more various, and fuller understanding of the ancient Greeks. It is not meant, of course, to serve as an exhaustive or complete picture of ancient Greek society. My presentation has been influenced by what I see as the glaring absences and misrepresentations, the narrowness and reduction of the conservative portraits of the Greeks I described earlier. In my view, the study of ancient culture presents a manifold, various, often contradictory and ambiguous repertory, a lost compendium of human practices, some of them cruel and brutal, some more utopian, more open, less contained, less controlled, and less "policed" than our own. The ancient Greeks were not just Athenians, not just philosophers in conversation. Representations of ancient Greek society in the contemporary public domain need to be liberated from the fatal embrace of neoconservative thought, which narcissistically sees the ancient world as identical to itself, as fully explained by narratives of nationalism, domestication and family values, militarism, patriarchy, and elitism. Ancient Greek society is *one* of the sources of contemporary culture, eminently worthy of being known and understood as such. It should be compelling study for contemporary Americans also because it was considered for centuries to be, along with ancient Israel, one of the only sources of Western civilization; this narrative of origins is deserving of our common interest as well. But even more, the Greeks are fascinating because they were not like us, because, although we owe to them some of the institutions through which we organize our own culture, they did it all quite differently, and therefore offer us difference from ourselves, other voices, latent traces of features of their culture filtered and edited out through centuries of interested inheritance. Let us, in the inexhaustible study of Greek antiquity, refuse the bowdlerizing of Greek myth, the heterosexualization of the ancient Athenians, the celebration or denunciation of ancient democracy, and read Sappho and Herodotus as well as Plato, recover unfamiliar traces of the ancient past such as a Greek delight in obscenity, the cultivation of multiple sexual differences, a world full of gods, and the political intensities of radical democracy.

Notes

1. William Bennett, *The Book of Virtues: A Treasury of Moral Stories* (New York, 1993), 211.

2. See Robert Koehler, "New Page for 'Book of Virtues,'" *Los Angeles Times,* September 2, 1996, F16.

3. William J. Bennett, *The Moral Compass: A Companion to the Book of Virtues: Stories for a Life's Journey,* ed. with commentary (New York, 1995), 322.

4. Jon Wiener, "The Olin Money Tree: Dollars for Neocon Scholars," *The Nation* 250:1 (January 1, 1990), 12; Eric Alterman, "The Troves of Academe," *The Nation* 262:25 (June 24,1996) 22. See also John M. Swomley, "Funding for the Culture War," *The Humanist* 56:3 (May/June 1996), 34–35. On the massive conservative apparatus of think tanks, training programs, foundations, and other institutions, see Ellen Messer-Davidow, "Manufacturing the Attack on Liberalized Higher Education," *Social Text* 36 (1993), 40–80.

5. Allan Bloom, *The Closing of the American Mind: How Higher Education Has Failed Democracy and Impoverished the Souls of Today's Students* (New York, 1987), 88.

6. Donald Kagan, *On the Origins of War and the Preservation of Peace* (New York, 1995).

7. Victor Davis Hanson, *Fields without Dreams: Defending the Agrarian Idea* (New York, 1996).

8. Camille Paglia, *Sexual Personae: Art and Decadence from Nefertiti to Emily Dickinson* (New Haven, 1990).

9. Martin Bernal, *Black Athena: The Afroasiatic Roots of Classical Civilization* (New Brunswick, 1987).

10. Lawrence L. Levine, *The Opening of the American Mind: Canons, Culture, and History* (Boston, 1996).

11. Mary Lefkowitz, *Not Out of Africa: How Afrocentrism Became an Excuse to Teach Myth as History* (New York, 1996), 50.

12. C. Loring Brace, with David P. Tracer, Lucia Allen Yaroch, John Robb, Kari Brandt, and A. Russell Nelson, "Clines and Clusters versus 'Race': A Test in Ancient Egypt and the Case of a Death on the Nile," in *Black Athena Revisited,* ed. Mary Lefkowitz and Guy MacLean Rogers (Chapel Hill and London, 1996), 158.

13. Paul Gilroy, *The Black Atlantic: Modernity and Double Consciousness* (Cambridge, Mass., 1993), 188.

14. Hanson, *Fields without Dreams,* x.

15. Donald Kagan, *Pericles of Athens and the Birth of Democracy* (New York, 1991), 260.

16. Aristotle, *Politics,* trans. H. Rackham (London, 1972).

17. Plato, *Collected Dialogues,* ed. Edith Hamilton and Huntington Cairns (Princeton, 1961).

18. *Sappho's Lyre: Archaic Lyric and Women Poets of Ancient Greece,* trans. Diane Rayor (Berkeley, 1991), 55.

19. Paglia, *Sexual Personae,* 38.

20. *The Homeric Hymns,* trans. Apostolos Athanassakis (Baltimore, 1976), 49. All quotations from the *Homeric Hymns* refer to this edition.

21. Plato, *Collected Dialogues.*

22. Plutarch, "Pelopidas," in *The Lives of the Noble Gre-*

cians and Romans, trans. John Dryden, rev. A. H. Clough (New York, n.d.), 356–57.

23. *Sappho's Lyre,* #19, p. 63.

24. Vincent Scully, *The Earth, The Temple, and the Gods: Greek Sacred Architecture,* rev. ed. (New Haven, 1979), 90–91.

More Reading

Beard, Mary, and John Henderson. *Classics: A Very Short Introduction* (Oxford, 1995).

Burkert, Walter. *Greek Religion* (Cambridge, Mass., 1985).

Carson, Anne. *Eros the Bittersweet: An Essay* (Princeton, 1986).

Cartledge, Paul. *The Greeks* (Oxford, 1993).

Detienne, Marcel. *The Gardens of Adonis: Spices in Greek Mythology,* trans. Janet Lloyd (Atlantic Highlands, N.J., 1977).

duBois, Page. *Sowing the Body: Psychoanalysis and Ancient Representations of Women* (Chicago, 1988).

———. *Sappho Is Burning* (Chicago, 1995).

Gentili, Bruno. *Poetry and Its Public in Ancient Greece,* trans. A. T. Cole (Baltimore, 1988).

Halperin, David. *One Hundred Years of Homosexuality and Other Essays on Greek Love* (New York, 1990).

Halperin, David, J. J. Winkler, and F. Zeitlin, eds. *Before Sexuality: The Construction of Erotic Experience in the Ancient Greek World* (Princeton, 1990).

Konstan, David. *Greek Comedy and Ideology* (New York, 1995).

Kurke, Leslie. *Coins, Bodies, Games and Gold: The Politics of Meaning in Archaic Greece* (Princeton, 1999).

Kurke, Leslie, and Carol Dougherty, eds. *Cultural Poetics in Archaic Greece: Cult, Performance, Politics* (Cambridge, 1993).

Lissarague, François. *The Aesthetics of the Greek Banquet: Images of Wine and Ritual,* trans. A. Szegedy-Maszak (Princeton, 1990).

Loraux, Nicole. *The Invention of Athens: The Funeral Oration in the Classical City,* trans. Alan Sheridan (Cambridge, Mass., 1986).

Morris, Sarah. *Daidalos and the Origins of Greek Art* (Princeton, 1992).

Nagy, Gregory. *The Best of the Achaeans: Concepts of the Hero in Archaic Greek Poetry* (Cambridge, Mass., 1979).

Ober, Josiah. *Mass and Elite in Democratic Athens: Rhetoric, Ideology, and the Power of the People* (Princeton, 1989).

Ober, Josiah, and Charles Hedrick, eds. *Demokratia: A Conversation on Democracies, Ancient and Modern* (Princeton, 1996).

Roberts, Jennifer Tolbert. *Athens on Trial: The Antidemocratic Tradition in Western Thought* (Princeton, 1994).

Rose, Peter. *Sons of the Gods, Children of Earth* (Ithaca, 1992).

Segal, Charles. *Interpreting Greek Tragedy: Myth, Poetry, Text* (Ithaca, 1986).

Selden, Daniel, and Ralph Hexter, eds. *Innovations of Antiquity* (New York, 1992).

Sissa, Giulia. *Greek Virginity,* trans. A. Goldhammer (Cambridge, Mass., 1990).

Vernant, Jean-Pierre. *Myth and Society in Ancient Greece,* trans. Janet Lloyd (Atlantic Highlands, N.J., 1980).

Winkler, John J., and Froma Zeitlin, eds. *Nothing to Do with*

Dionysos? Athenian Drama in Its Social Context (Princeton, 1990).

Zeitlin, Froma. *Playing the Other: Gender and Society in Classical Greek Literature* (Chicago, 1996).

Index

About the Author

Page duBois is Professor of Classics and Cultural Studies at the University of California, San Diego. Her books include *Sappho Is Burning, Torture and Truth, Sowing the Body: Psychoanalysis and Ancient Representations of Women,* and *Centaurs and Amazons: Women and the Pre-History of the Great Chain of Being.*

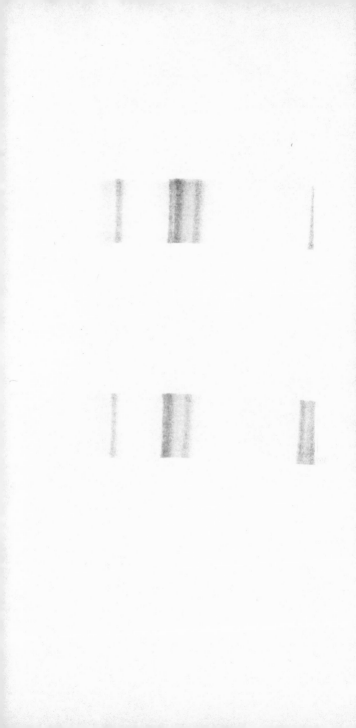